3

Writing to Communicate

Essays and the Short Research Paper

Cynthia A. Boardman

Spring International Learning Center
University of Arkansas, Fayetteville

PEARSON
Longman

Writing to Communicate 3: Essays and the Short Research Paper

Pearson Education, 10 Bank Street, White Plains, NY 10606

Staff credits: The people who made up the *Writing to Communicate 3: Essays and the Short Research Paper* team, representing editorial, production, design, and manufacturing, are Pietro Alongi, Wendy Campbell, Rosa M. Chapinal, Ann France, Edith Pullman, Jennifer Stem, Paula Van Ells, and Dorothy Zemach.

Cover photo: Momatiuk Eastcott/Corbis
Text art and composition: S4Carlisle Publishing Services
Text font: 11.5/13 Minion
Illustrations: Steve Schulman

Text Credits:
p. 59-60, "He Says, She Says" by Erin Allday, Courtesy of the *San Francisco Chronicle*, Hearst Corporation, 2007; **p. 68,** "Girls Really do Prefer Pink" by Ed Edelson, August 2007, Copyright © 2007 Scout News, LLC. All rights reserved; **p. 86,** *The Matter of Kindness,* reproduced with permission from *The Kindness of Strangers*, Lonely Planet, © 2003 Lonely Planet Publications; **p. 90,** "Schools Playing Down Valedictorian Honors" by Marissa DeCuir, USA Today, June 28, 2007, reprinted with permission; **p. 91,** "Preserve the Valedictorian Tradition" by Eric Effron, *The Week*, June 22, 2007; **p. 99,** "One high school – 44 valedictorians" by Lynn Thompson, Copyright 2005, Seattle Times Company. Used with permission; **p. 103-104,** "I'm just sayin'" by Greg Sellnow, *Post-Bulletin*, September 8, 2007; **p. 104-105,** "Not all Gen Y'ers are spoiled brats: What the study on narcissistic twentysomethings really reveals" by Sara Libby, *Los Angeles Times*, March 2, 2007; **p. 142,** "Zolpidem," Copyright 2008, American Society of Health System-Pharmacists, Bethesda, MD., www.ashp.org. Used with permission.

Photo Credits:
p. xiv © Richard T. Nowitz/Corbis; **p. 1** Thomas M. Perkins/Shutterstock; **p. 2** © Francis G. Mayer/Corbis; **p. 14** music Alan King/Alamy; **p. 21** © Sven Hagolani/zefa/Corbis; **p. 36** © Chuck Savage/Corbis; **p. 48** photo create/Shutterstock; **p. 52** © Fabrizio Bensch/Reuters/Corbis; **p. 53** Thomas M. Perkins/ Shutterstock; **p. 54** Donna Day/Stone Collection/Getty Images; **p. 70** David Noble Photography/Alamy; **p. 88** moodboard/Alamy; **p. 90** © Comstock Images; **p. 99** Mark Bonham/Shutterstock; **p. 110** digital skillet/Shutterstock; **p. 111** Markabond/Shutterstock; **p. 112** Mira/Alamy; **p. 118** imagebroker/Alamy; **p. 123** © Juice Images Limited/Alamy; **p. 126** © Jose Luis Pelaez, Inc./Corbis; **p. 129** Associated Press/ Giovanni Diffidenti/AP Images; **p. 137** icyimage/Shutterstock Images LLC.

Library of Congress Cataloging-in-Publication Data
Boardman, Cynthia A.
   Writing to communicate. book 3: essays and the short research paper/Cynthia Boardman.
      p. cm.
   ISBN 978-0-13-240744-1 (student text bk. : alk. paper)—ISBN 978-0-13-240745-8 (answer key : alk. paper) 1. English language—Textbooks for foreign speakers. 2. English language—Paragraphs—Problems, exercises, etc. 3. English language—Essays —Problems, exercises, etc. 4. English language—Rhetoric—Problems, exercises, etc. I. Title.
   PE1128.B5939 2008
   808'.042—dc22

                                                                2008024758

ISBN-10: 0-13-240744-2
ISBN-13: 978-0-13-240744-1

Printed in the United States of America
2 3 4 5 6 7 8 9 10—DEL—11 10 09

DEDICATION

To Ed, for his love, patience, and good cooking

ACKNOWLEDGMENTS

In my twenty-nine (and counting) years in the field of teaching English as a Second Language, there have been many, many people who have contributed to my understanding and development as a teacher—far too many people to name. However, I do want to acknowledge what I owe to my professors, colleagues, and countless students. Professors have inspired me, colleagues have encouraged me, and students from different continents communicating with one another and learning to appreciate one another's countries have brought me the hope that maybe there is a chance for peace after all.

I thank Jia Frydenberg for the countless hours she spent discussing the contents of this book with me. Her input was invaluable in the early drafts of many chapters.

In addition, without the many contributions of Laura Le Dréan and Dorothy Zemach, this book could not have been written, and I am truly grateful to them. An additional tip of the hat goes to Dorothy Zemach for being the best development editor in the business, in my humble opinion.

Finally, I wish to extend many thanks to the people at Pearson Education for their efforts in this project: Pietro Alongi, Wendy Campbell, Rosa M. Chapinal, Ann France, Edith Pullman, Jennifer Stem, and Paula Van Ells.

Cynthia A. Boardman

CONTENTS

CHAPTER 6 TWO SIDES OF AN ISSUE: RESPONDING
WITH PARAPHRASING 88
Generation Y: Hardworking or Spoiled?

CHAPTER 7 THE FIRST DRAFT 112
Sleep

CHAPTER 8 DOING RESEARCH 126
Sleeping Pills

TO THE TEACHER

Introduction

Welcome to the third book in the *Writing to Communicate* series. With the addition of this book, *Essays and the Short Research Paper*, the series covers the spectrum of academic writing from writing paragraphs at a high beginning/low intermediate proficiency level to writing a short research paper at the high intermediate/low advanced proficiency level. Just as *WTC2* takes a step-by-step approach to the expansion of a paragraph to an essay, *WTC3* takes a step-by-step approach to writing a personal experience essay to writing with support from outside sources. It is this step-by-step approach that has, in my view, led to the success of *WTC2,* and I believe it will prove to be equally successful for students and teachers who use *WTC3*.

This book briefly reviews the basic tenets of paragraph and essay organization and then moves on to the components needed to be successful at incorporating outside support into an essay. These lessons are preparatory for the final writing assignment: a short research paper.

In addition, like Books 1 and 2, Book 3 includes an introduction to various organizational patterns in different world languages (based on Robert Kaplan's brilliant first work on contrastive analysis "Cultural thought patterns in intercultural education."). Likewise, the "Bringing It All Together" section after each part of the book reviews important organizational structures and language.

The Chapters

- **Part I: Writing Academic Essays** Chapter 1 reviews the most salient aspects of paragraph and essay structure as well as the process of writing. Chapters 2 and 3 focus on two rhetorical patterns not covered in *WTC2*: cause/effect and problem/solution.

- **Part II: Reading and Responding** This part takes up the ways in which outside sources can be incorporated into an essay. Chapter 4 covers summary writing; Chapter 5, quoting; and Chapter 6, paraphrasing. Each of these chapters contains excerpts from articles and books, many of which have been adapted to make them readily accessible to students at the high intermediate/low advanced proficiency levels.

- **Part III: The Short Research Paper** This part takes students step-by-step through the process of writing a short research paper. As this part of the book moves through each step with its topic (sleep), students follow along using their own topics. Chapter 7 takes them through writing the first draft. Chapter 8 shows them how to find and where to add concrete support to create the second draft. Chapter 9 demonstrates revising and editing techniques and research paper format. By the end of this chapter, students have completed their own research paper.

Chapter Organization

Each chapter is divided into four sections: Writing Focus, Sentence Focus, Language Focus, and Writing to Communicate.

Writing Focus introduces the major writing focus for the chapter and offers plenty of practice exercises. **Sentence Focus** covers difficult grammatical structures and common sentence-level mistakes. Some Sentence Focus sections coordinate with the topic of the Writing Focus topic for that chapter. **Language Focus** deals with various vocabulary concerns, many of which go hand-in-hand with the Writing Focus topic. There are also Language Focus sections that list commonly confused words and their correct usage. Explanations are followed by practice exercises. **Writing to Communicate** is similar to what it is in the other books: It presents a writing assignment, a peer help worksheet, and additional topics for writing either journal entries or essays.

Audience

The book is intended to fit into the higher levels of a writing program that guides students from beginning to advanced academic writing of English at the college level. It is expected that students who use this book have had some previous experience with writing paragraph and essay-length compositions, as well as some exposure to the rhetorical structure of paragraphs and essays. In addition, students who have fairly good reading skills will find an easier time using this book and doing the research required. English as a Second Language students usually score in the 60-80 range of the Internet-based TOEFL® (iBT) or 497-550 on the paper-based TOEFL. However, higher-level ESL students as well as native speakers who have not previously studied research paper writing will equally benefit from the information and practice in this book.

Appendices

There are six appendices, all of which can be copied for classroom use. Five of these are similar to those in *WTC2*: Essay Format, Common Connectors, The Writing Process, General Peer Help Worksheet, and Evaluation Rubrics. The last appendix is an overview of MLA documentation. Since the chapters themselves instruct students on the APA style of formatting, the MLA style is offered here for those teachers and students who prefer it.

Answer Key

You can request a separate Answer Key from Pearson, Inc. by calling or e-mailing the Pearson representative in your country.

Questions and Comments

I welcome your comments and suggestions to this edition of *Writing to Communicate 3: Essays and the Short Research Paper*. Please contact me through Pearson Education, 10 Bank Street, White Plains, New York 10606.

July 2008

Cynthia A. Boardman

TO THE STUDENT

Welcome to *Writing to Communicate 3: Essays and the Short Research Paper*. With this book, you will review paragraph and essay writing and then learn how to write a short documented research paper. Writing term papers will be a major part of your university experience, and it is important to learn how they are done so that you can give your instructors the type of paper that they are expecting.

Like all writing, the research paper assignment is a process that has many stages. It starts with an idea that you are interested in exploring. From there, you organize the paper, find outside sources to support your ideas, incorporate information from these sources into your paper in appropriate ways, and then present the paper in the appropriate format. This process is cyclical, and since being a good writer means you continually change, add to, and improve what you have already written, you may find that it is necessary to repeat certain steps.

In addition to writing a research paper, you will also learn to avoid common sentence-level mistakes and will practice various grammatical structures that make your writing more sophisticated. Several sections on vocabulary will allow you to understand the nuances of certain words and their correct usage. Finally, a part at the end of each chapter offers other avenues for you to improve your writing by making journal entries or by writing another academic assignment.

In short, once you complete the assignments in this book, you will be ready to tackle the writing assignments that you will receive in your academic classes. I hope that your experience with *Writing to Communicate 3: Essays and the Short Research Paper* is both a valuable and an interesting one.

Cynthia A. Boardman

INTRODUCTION: WRITING IN ENGLISH

Writing to communicate dates back thousands of years. Writing started as symbols on a cave wall, and then, about 3500 years ago, the idea of an alphabet developed. Today there are about 20 major alphabets used to communicate in the world's languages.

In addition to using different alphabets, languages also use different writing styles of organization.* English organization, for example, is fairly simple. English uses a straight line from beginning to end. When English speakers read an article, they expect the article to have a beginning, a middle, and an end. The beginning should say what the article is going to be about, the middle should talk about the topic of the article, and the end should say what the article was about. Here is a diagram of the English style of writing.

> This is what I will write about.
>
> I am writing about it here.
>
> This is what I wrote about.

Diagram 1: English Organization

*Kaplan, R. B. "Cultural thought patterns in intercultural education." *Language Learning, 16*(1), 1966.

Other languages organize writing differently. For example, Spanish organization is similar to English, but the line from beginning to end isn't so straight. Spanish speakers write about the topic, but here and there they add something that is not directly related to the topic. To a Spanish speaker, this makes the writing more interesting. Here is a diagram of the Spanish style of writing.

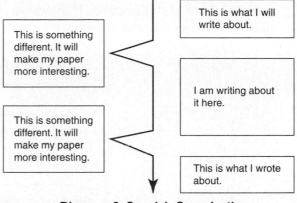

Diagram 2: Spanish Organization

The Japanese style of writing is often circular. This means that the topic comes at the end of the article. In fact, sometimes, the writer doesn't say what the topic is. Instead, he gives hints to help the reader guess the topic. Here is a diagram of the Japanese style of writing.

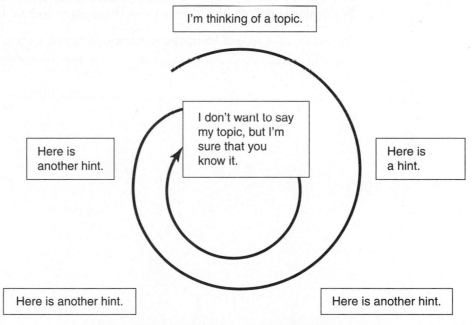

Diagram 3: Japanese Organization

Still another style of writing is used in Arabic. To be a good writer in Arabic, you need to write in a parallel style. This means that you write using coordinating conjunctions, such as *and, or,* or *but.* English, on the other hand, uses more subordinating conjunctions, such as *when*, *before*, or *until.* Arabic writing is also more repetitive than English writing. To an English reader, this coordination and repetition would be boring, but to an Arabic reader, this style is elegant and what is expected. Look at this diagram. It shows the repetition and coordination that is necessary for good Arabic writing.

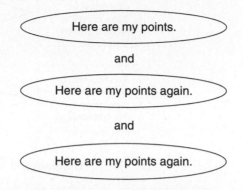

Here are my points.

and

Here are my points again.

and

Here are my points again.

Diagram 4: Arabic Organization

The most important idea here is one style of writing isn't better than another, just as one language isn't better than another. The styles are just different. To be a successful writer in any language, you need to learn the writing style of that particular language in addition to its vocabulary and its grammar rules.

In this book, you will learn the **American English** style of writing.

WRITING ACADEMIC ESSAYS

THE PROCESS OF WRITING

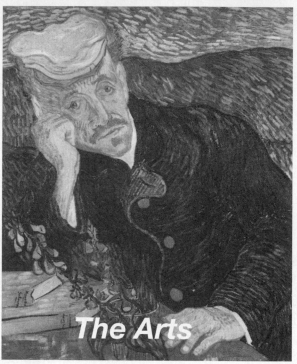

The Arts

Portrait of Dr. Gachet
by Vincent Van Gogh

I WRITING FOCUS

Imagine that you have just entered your first class in a college or university, and you have just been given your first homework assignment, which is to write an essay that is due in two days. How do you handle this assignment?

If you are not sure, you may be surprised to discover that your classmates may be equally uncertain. Written language is different from spoken language, and essay writing is a particular form of written language with its own style and organization. In addition, different languages are organized differently in writing. Therefore, both native speakers and non-native speakers have to learn how to write in academic English.

It is important to learn the English academic style of writing because this is the type of organization that your professor will be expecting. The **paragraph** is the basic unit of organization. Once you know how to write an academic paragraph, you can easily expand that knowledge to write **essays** and **research papers**.

What about you?

Do you like to write? What kind of writing? Have you written essays in English before? Share your answers with a classmate.

Paragraph Organization

Most of the paragraphs that you write will be for the body of an essay. These paragraphs typically have three parts: the **topic sentence, the body**, and the **concluding sentence**.

The Topic Sentence

The topic sentence controls the paragraph and contains its main idea. It should have a **topic** (what you are talking about) and a **controlling idea** (what you are saying about the topic). For example:

➤ Music plays an important role in my life.
    topic   controlling idea

Topic sentences usually come at the beginning of a paragraph, but they may follow an introductory sentence as well. When this is the case, you may need to add a connecting word or phrase that relates the two sentences. For example:

➤ I can't play an instrument or carry a tune. Still, music plays
       Introductory sentence.   Connection,

an important role in my life.
      topic sentence.

➤ Most high school students have no interest in poetry. However,
         Introductory sentence.   Connection,

using song lyrics, which are a type of poetry, is a good way to teach them
          topic sentence.

the basics of poetic style.

➤ Before I hired a landscape architect, I thought that a backyard was fine if it
         Introductory sentence.

had a lawn and a couple of trees. Now I know that a landscape architect is
         Connection   topic sentence.

truly an artist.

■ **PRACTICE 1: Connecting Introductory Sentences to Topic Sentences**

Each item below has several parts. Rearrange the parts to make two sentences: an introductory sentence and a topic sentence. Then underline the connection between the two sentences. Compare your answers with a classmate.

1. but a really good museum is hard to find
in order to be considered exceptional
museums are everywhere
museums must have three qualities

_____

_____

_____

2. and entertained themselves with drums
for example
fought with drums
people have communicated with drums
people have used drums
throughout history

_____

_____

_____

3. the pennywhistle and the accordion

have become two well-known Irish instruments

is a blend of many special instruments

because of their unique ability to blend with other instruments

if you listen to Irish music

you can appreciate that its sound

_____

_____

_____

4. are necessary for artistic genius

at least three personality traits

however, it seems

it's hard to identify what makes artistic genius

_____

_____

_____

5. is to be creative on the spot

no musicians improvise as well as jazz musicians

the definition of improvisation

while many musicians improvise

_____

_____

_____

The Body

The body of a paragraph contains support for the topic sentence, such as explanations, examples, and reasons. Structurally, the body generally consists of two types of **supporting sentences:**

- **major supporting sentences**

  These directly support the topic sentence.

- **minor supporting sentences**

  These support the major supporting sentence that precedes them.

The Concluding Sentence

The concluding sentence ends the paragraph. It reminds the reader of the paragraph's content by restating the topic sentence or summarizing the supporting sentences. In a stand-alone paragraph, you should write a concluding sentence. In an essay, however, it is not always necessary.

■ PRACTICE 2: **Identifying the Parts of a Paragraph**

Read the body of the paragraph below. Then check (✓) the box of the best topic sentence and the best concluding sentence.

The Traditional Music of the United States

❏ There are many kinds of music in the United States.

❏ Jazz, country, and folk are three types of traditional music of the United States.

❏ The history of the United States is reflected in its music.

　　Jazz, the first type of traditional music in the United States, was born when the music of Africa blended with the music of Europe. Beginning in the seventeenth century, African people were brought to North America to be slaves. The European slave owners didn't allow the Africans to play their own music, so the slaves incorporated European harmonies and melodies into the familiar music of their native land. The second type of traditional music, country, reflects the immigrant "melting pot" of the population of the United States. It developed from the Irish and English immigrants that settled in the Appalachian Mountains in the east. The third type of traditional music, folk music, can be characterized by its acoustic[1] guitars and its singers' voices. The height of its popularity occurred in the 1950s and 1960s, when many singers wrote and sang songs to protest against war, discrimination, and injustice.

❏ In conclusion, music is an important part of the history of the United States.

❏ All in all, the best type of traditional music in the United States is jazz.

❏ In short, these three types of music make up the traditional music of the United States.

---

[1]**acoustic** *adj.* not having the music from an instrument made louder electronically through amplifiers

Outlining a Paragraph

Outlining a paragraph clearly shows the relationship among the parts of the paragraph and between the sentences. Study the outline on page 6 to understand the relationship among the sentences in a typical paragraph. Notice that an introductory sentence before the topic sentence is not outlined.

Model Paragraph Outline

    I. Jazz, country, and folk . . .   (topic sentence)

        A. Jazz, the first . . .   (major support)

            1. Beginning in . . .   (minor support)

            2. The European . . .   (minor support)

        B. The second type . . .   (major support)

            1. It developed . . .   (minor support)

        C. The third type . . .   (major support)

            1. The height of its . . .   (minor support)

   II. In short, . . .   (concluding sentence)

■ PRACTICE 3: **Analyzing a Paragraph**

Analyze the paragraph below first by identifying the topic sentence and then by outlining it on a separate piece of paper. You do not need to include the introductory sentence, if there is one.

The Hard Life of a Ballet Dancer

Children who watch a ballet performance may have romantic dreams of the glamorous lives of the dancers. However, ballet dancers have difficult lives. Their careers start at a very young age. Child dancers are expected to practice for hours  after school each day and on weekends. They are discouraged from participating in any school activities. After high school, the young adults may be lucky enough to get a job as a ballet dancer. However, there are far more dancers than there are full-time jobs, so many dancers are disappointed. They may have to make a living by working in several part-time ballet jobs at first. Once dancers are employed by a ballet company full-time, the work and practice only get harder. The dancers' everyday schedule is very demanding, and they get little time off. Then, after ten or fifteen years of dancing, they must retire since most ballet companies don't want dancers who are older than 35. However, ballet is all that they know. It becomes difficult to refocus their lives on teaching or on finding another career. In short, the life of a ballet dancer is not an easy one.

■ *PRACTICE 4*: **Writing a Paragraph**

Write a paragraph about the role that music plays in your life. Follow this procedure:

1. **Brainstorm** about the ways that music is in your life by talking with a partner or thinking by yourself. For example, do you play an instrument? Do you listen to music? Why? When? How often? What kind? Where? Write your notes on another piece of paper.

2. **Organize** your ideas into a paragraph outline. First, write your topic sentence. Answer this question to help formulate your topic sentence: "What role does music play in my life?" Possible topic sentences include:
   - Music is the most important part of my life.
   - Music isn't a very big part of my life.
   - I couldn't live without music in my life.

I. Your topic sentence: _____

   _____

   A. First main point: _____
      1. explanation or example: _____

         _____

      2. explanation or example: _____

         _____

   B. Second main point: _____
      1. explanation or example: _____

         _____

      2. explanation or example: _____

         _____

   C. Third main point: _____
      1. explanation or example: _____

         _____

      2. explanation or example: _____

         _____

II. Your concluding sentence: _____

   _____

3. **Write your paragraph** using good paragraph format (title, indentation, double spacing, and so on). See Appendix 1 on page 163 for more on paragraph formatting.

Essay Organization

In a university class, you will usually need to write more than a paragraph to present all of your information. Expanding a paragraph into an essay is easy now that you have a clear understanding of how to organize a paragraph. Like a paragraph, an essay has three parts:

- **the introductory paragraph**
- **body paragraphs**
- **the concluding paragraph**

While the introductory and concluding paragraphs have different organizational patterns, the body paragraphs are basically organized like the individual paragraphs you studied earlier in this chapter. Look at the diagram below. It shows how the model paragraph is expanded into an essay so that more information can be included.

Expansion of a Paragraph into an Essay

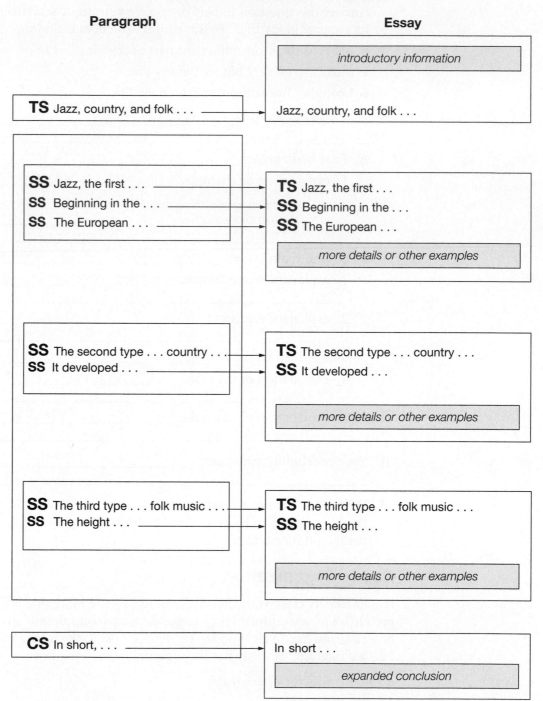

The Introductory Paragraph

The introductory paragraph gets your reader interested in your essay and presents your main idea—in that order.

Use a **hook** to get your reader interested in your essay. Common hooks are:

- **general to specific**

  Start with a broad topic and narrow it down to a manageable topic for an essay.

- **a short anecdote**

  Write a personal story that relates to your topic.

- **a historical introduction**

  Write a brief history of your topic.

At the end of an introductory paragraph is the **thesis statement**. Like a topic sentence, a thesis statement expresses the main idea of the essay, and it has a topic and controlling idea. It must also show a clear intent or opinion. For example:

> ➤ There are <u>three types</u> of <u>traditional music in the United States</u>.
>   controlling idea   topic
>   showing intent

> ➤ <u>A ballet dancer</u> <u>has a difficult life</u>.
>   topic   controlling idea
>   showing opinion

In addition, many thesis statements have a **predictor**. This is an extra part of the thesis statement that can predict the number and content of the body paragraphs. In the following example, the predictor has been boxed.

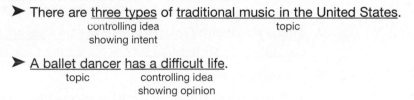

> ➤ Vincent Van Gogh has remained a popular artist because of the vibrancy of the colors in his paintings, the boldness of his brushstrokes, and the tragedy of his life story.

From this thesis, the reader can predict that the essay will have three body paragraphs:

- The first will be about the colors in Van Gogh's paintings.

- The second will be about his brushstrokes.

- The third will be about Van Gogh's life.

■ PRACTICE 5: Analyzing Thesis Statements

For each thesis statement, circle the topic, underline the controlling idea, and put a box around the predictors, if any.

1. The Pyramids of Egypt, the Great Wall of China, and the city at Machu Picchu are all reflections of the societies that built them.

2. The rhythms of South American music have produced the tango, the samba, and the salsa dance styles.

3. Fashion is an important part of cultural expression.

4. The study of literature can be divided into four areas: poetry, prose, essay, and drama.

(continued)

5. Singing, acting, dancing, and scenery combine to tell a story in a typical Italian opera.

6. Photography is the most appealing visual art.

■ PRACTICE 6: Writing Thesis Statements

Practice writing thesis statements by answering these questions. Then put some of the answers together to make a thesis statement. Include a predictor if you like.

1. A particular type of music

   What is a kind of music that you know about and enjoy? Where does it come from? What is special about it?

   a. Topic: *Hawaiian music*

The name of the music

   b. Controlling idea: *not like music in other states*

What you want to say about this music

   c. Predictor: *ethnic Hawaiian and Jawaiian (a blend of Jamaican and Hawaiian music)*

A division you want to emphasize

   d. Thesis statement: *Ethnic Hawaiian and Jawaiian are two types of Hawaiian music that are unlike any music in the rest of the United States.*

2. Your favorite type of art

   What is your favorite type of art? Painting? Photography? Sculpture? Crafts (pottery, weaving)? What do you like about it? Do you admire it or produce it?

   a. Topic: _____

The name of the art

   b. Controlling idea: _____

   c. Predictor: _____

   _____

   d. Thesis statement: _____

   _____

   _____

3. Your favorite type of entertainment

   What entertains you? Movies? Sports? Parties? Computer games? Do you like to participate or watch?

   a. Topic: _____

The name of the type of entertainment

   b. Controlling idea: _____

   c. Predictor: _____

   _____

   d. Thesis statement: _____

   _____

   _____

4. A musical instrument you know how to play

   Do you play a musical instrument? What is it? When did you start playing? Why do you like playing it? Did you use to play an instrument? Why did you stop?

   a. Topic: _____
   The name of the instrument

   b. Controlling idea: _____

   c. Predictor: _____

   _____

   d. Thesis statement: _____

   _____

   _____

5. A famous entertainer

   Who is the entertainer? What does this person do to entertain? Why do you like/dislike him or her?

   a. Topic: _____
   The name of the entertainer

   b. Controlling idea: _____

   c. Predictor: _____

   _____

   d. Thesis statement: _____

   _____

   _____

Body Paragraphs

As mentioned previously, the body paragraphs of an essay are usually organized with a topic sentence, supporting sentences, and a concluding sentence. However, there are some possible variations. Since the main idea of an essay and the intent and/or opinion are contained in the thesis statement, a topic sentence is not always necessary in each body paragraph. This is especially true when the thesis statement has a predictor. Similarly, having a concluding sentence in each body paragraph is optional.

Instead of being a topic sentence, the first sentence in a body paragraph may function as a transition, or **bridge**, to the next paragraph. Also, instead of a concluding sentence, you could use a bridge as a transition to the next body paragraph. Read the following essay. Notice the bridges, which are underlined.

The Traditional Music of the United States

What music truly belongs to one country? The traditional music of a country is becoming difficult to identify in this age of globalization. Still, there are rhythms, instruments, and melodies that seem to be uniquely Chinese or African or Jamaican. Even though it is a young country, the United States has also given birth to some unique musical styles. For example, jazz, country, and folk are three types of traditional music of the United States.

Jazz, the first type of traditional music in the United States, was born when the music of Africa blended with the music of Europe. Beginning in the seventeenth century, African people were brought to North America to be slaves. The Africans remembered their music, but the European slave owners didn't allow the Africans to play their own music. Therefore, the slaves incorporated European harmonies and melodies into the familiar music of their native land. <u>However, jazz isn't the only music that developed from music brought from other lands</u>.
bridge

The second type of traditional music, country, reflects the immigrant "melting pot" of the population of the United States. It developed from the Irish and English that settled in the Appalachian Mountains. As different immigrant populations arrived, sounds of different countries were added to the mix. Country music is characterized by steel guitars and powerful harmonies. The best-known type of country music comes from Nashville in Tennessee, where the Grand Ole Opry is located. Country music stars come to this concert hall and perform for enthusiastic audiences. The show is broadcast via radio. Because of this broadcast, the sound of country music has been spread to the rest of the United States and beyond.

<u>Radio also helped spread the third type of traditional music.</u> Folk music can
bridge
be characterized by its acoustic guitars and its singers' voices. It gained national recognition in the 1930s and 1940s with such singers as Woody Guthrie and Pete Seeger. The height of its popularity occurred in the 1950s and 1960s, when many singers wrote and sang songs to protest against war, discrimination, and injustice. Performers like Bob Dylan and Joan Baez brought people together in their commitment to making the world a better place.

In conclusion, the traditional music of the United States is like the traditional music of any country because it developed from the experiences of its people. Jazz came from the enslavement of African people, country music came from the mixing of immigrants from many nations, and folk music came from the blending of an acoustic guitar and a human voice.

What about you?

Is music important to you? Why or why not? Share your answer with a classmate.

■ *PRACTICE 7:* **Completing an Essay**

Complete this essay by writing a topic sentence or a bridge in the spaces provided.

Vincent Van Gogh

In 1990, a Japanese art dealer surprised the art world by purchasing Vincent Van Gogh's portrait of Dr. Gachet for the amazing price of $82.5 million. If he were alive, Van Gogh would be the most surprised of all by this sale and by his continuing popularity more than 100 years after his death. However, his enduring fame is not unjustified. Vincent Van Gogh has remained a popular artist because of the vibrancy of color in his paintings, the boldness of his brushstrokes, and the tragedy of his life story.

_____ He liked
topic sentence

to use bright colors that overemphasized the colors in the real world. For example, the yellows of his sunflowers are more intense than the yellows of real sunflowers. Another good example is his *Starry Night* painting. The moon is brighter than any sun would be, and the stars are almost as bright. In this painting, Van Gogh was emphasizing the amazing clarity of a starry night.

_____
bridge

Another reason for Van Gogh's enduring popularity is the boldness of his brushstrokes. It's easy to get lost in the swirls and circles of the background of one of his portrait paintings. Moreover, by looking closely at one of his paintings of wheat fields, you can see how confidently he painted short strokes in all the yellow-hued colors. Then, if you step back, you can see how hypnotizing the effect is. By looking at his paintings, you realize the strength he had as a painter.

_____ During his life, Van
bridge

Gogh painted thousands of paintings, but he wasn't successful at making a living at it. His brother supported him most of his life. Van Gogh also struggled his entire life to remain sane, and sometimes he did not succeed. It is well known that in one of his states of madness, he cut off part of his ear. He also spent time in a mental hospital in France, where he was treated for depression. The final tragedy of his life was dying by his own hand in a deeply depressed state.

In conclusion, Vincent Van Gogh is beloved as a painter after so many years because the colors and brushstrokes that characterize his paintings urge the viewer to look more closely and see the brilliance of his work. Unhappily, he is also remembered because of the sadness of his life. The greatest sadness, of course, is that he never knew what an enduring body of work he left behind.

The Concluding Paragraph

The concluding paragraph should leave the reader with a clear understanding of what the essay is about. You can do that by:

- writing a **restatement** of the thesis statement.

- writing a **summary** of the main points in the body paragraphs.

- writing a **final comment**. A final comment is one last thought that you want to leave your reader with. This can often be the most effective part of a concluding paragraph.

Since a paragraph is more than one sentence, you can include one or more of these parts. In fact, you can include them all. Look again at the concluding paragraph in the model essay. What parts does it have?

II SENTENCE FOCUS

Avoiding Choppy Sentences

As discussed previously, you can make your writing better by using good organization. Equally as important is to make logical connections between ideas within a paragraph. Ideas in sentences can be connected by combining two sentences to make a **compound sentence**. Several sentences in a row without these connections are called **choppy sentences**. For example, the passage below is considered choppy because the sentences are not connected to each other.

> The *didgeridoo* is an Australian aboriginal instrument. It is considered the oldest of the wind instruments. Players of the didgeridoo seem to snore less. Doctors have found scientific proof that this is true. Didgeridoo players breathe in a special way. They open up their air passage. They snore less.

Here is the passage again with the addition of **coordinating conjunctions** and **transitions**. It is clear that the sentences are better connected to each other and, therefore, less choppy.

> The *didgeridoo* is an Australian aboriginal instrument, **and** it is considered the oldest of the wind instruments. **Moreover,** players of the didgeridoo seem to snore less. **Indeed,** doctors have found scientific proof that this is true. Didgeridoo players breathe in a special way. They open up their air passage, **so** they snore less.

Using Coordinating Conjunctions and Transitions

Didgeridoo

Coordinating conjunctions and transitions connect sentences by showing the reader how the two are related. On page 15 is a table that lists some common coordinating conjunctions and transitions. (For a more complete list, see Appendix 2 on pages 164–165.)

	Addition	Chronology	Contrast	Emphasis	Example	Result
Transitions	furthermore in addition moreover	first second next then after that later on	however in contrast	indeed in fact	for example for instance	as a result consequently therefore
Coordinating Conjunctions	and		but yet			so

- When a coordinating conjunction combines two sentences, you need a comma before it.

  ➤ They open up their air passage, **so** they snore less.

- A comma follows a transition as well.

  ➤ They open up their air passage. **Therefore,** they snore less.

- Another common punctuation pattern with transitions uses a **semicolon** instead of a period. A writer uses a semicolon instead of a period to show a closer relationship between the two sentences.

  ➤ They open up their air passage; **therefore,** they snore less.

■ PRACTICE 8: Improving Choppy Sentences

Rewrite each of the passages below to make them less choppy. Use transitions and coordinating conjunctions. Then compare your new sentences with a classmate.

1. I was in New York. I wanted to see a play on Broadway. All of the shows were sold out. I went to a movie.

2. A new Hollywood movie opens on Friday. It stars Anthony Hopkins. He is a very good actor. He gets lots of acting jobs. He makes a lot of money.

3. Architects design buildings. They do much more. They see a building project through from beginning to end.

4. I was shopping for a house. I looked everywhere for one that I liked. I looked downtown. I looked at the beach. I looked in the suburbs. I found one at the beach that I liked. I made an appointment to see it. I loved the inside of the house as much as I liked the outside. I bought it.

5. Reggae music developed in Jamaica. It was not known in other countries. Bob Marley released his first album. It attracted international audiences. Reggae is now a very popular type of music throughout the world.

Using Participles as Adjectives

In addition to good organization and good sentence structure, using words and their varying forms well can also increase the quality of your writing. Adjectives in particular can add interesting information to a sentence.

The **present participle** of a verb can be used as an adjective. When it is, the adjective modifies the "doer" of the action. For example:

➤ The song <u>interests</u> the teenager. → the <u>interesting</u> song

In this example, the song is "doing" the action, so the present participle describes the song.

The **past participle** of a verb can also be used as an adjective. This kind of adjective modifies the "receiver" of the action of the verb. For example:

➤ The song <u>intrigues</u> the teenager. → The <u>intrigued</u> teenager

In this example, the teenager is receiving the action of the verb, so the past participle is used to describe him or her.

■ PRACTICE 9: Using Participles as Adjectives

A. Choose the correct participle of the verb in parentheses in the paragraph below. In some cases, either participle could work, but the meaning is different. Be prepared to explain the differences.

People-Watching at the Art Gallery

I had fun watching people in the Impressionist room in the art gallery last

week. To my right, a _____ woman studied a _____
(1. fascinating / fascinated)   (2. striking / struck)

painting. In front of me, an _____ father was trying to explain the
(3. irritating / irritated)

difference between Impressionism and Post-Impressionism to his

_____ daughter. To my left, a tour guide was explaining a
(4. boring / bored)

_____ image in a painting to a group of _____ French
(5. disturbing / disturbed)   (6. captivating / captivated)

tourists. One of the teenagers, however, seemed more _____ by the
(7. enchanting / enchanted)

two American teenage girls than he was by the painting. When I got

up to leave, I wondered how many people had been watching me while I was

watching them.

B. For each item in Part A, write a sentence in which the adjective becomes a verb.

1. *The painting fascinated the woman.* _____

2. _____

3. _____

4. _____

5. _____

6. _____

7. _____

IV WRITING TO COMMUNICATE

Your Turn

Successful writers go through a series of steps, called the **writing process**, in order to produce a good composition. (For a more detailed discussion of the writing process, see Appendix 3 on page 166.) Read the assignment, and then follow the steps of the writing process to complete it.

Write an essay on one of the topics below (from Practice 6). For this essay, you should not do any research. Write about what you already know.

1. a particular type of music
2. your favorite type of music or art
3. your favorite type of entertainment
4. the musical instrument that you play or the art that you create
5. a famous entertainer

Step 1: Understanding the Assignment

Before you begin, be sure that you understand the details of the assignment. With a classmate, discuss the answers to these questions about the assignment. If there are any questions you can't answer, ask your instructor.

- What is the topic of the paper?

- Why am I writing it?

- Where does the information for the paper come from?

- How long should it be?

- When is it due?

- How should I submit it?

Step 2: Brainstorming

One common way of brainstorming is to use a circle diagram. To brainstorm for this essay, use a diagram similar to the one illustrated here about the Vincent Van Gogh essay. Write your diagram on a separate piece of paper.

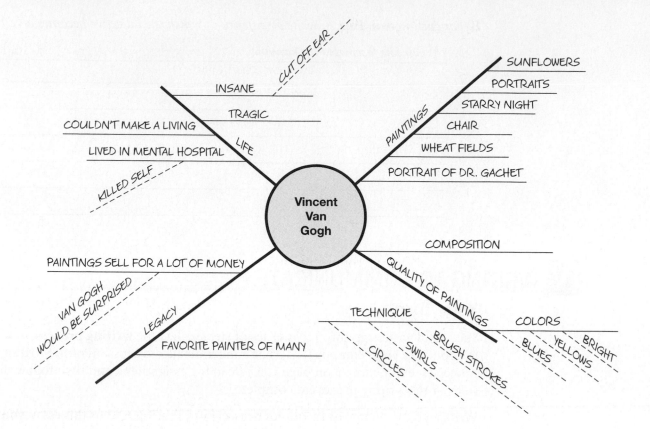

- Write your topic in the middle.

- On each thick line, write the main ideas that stem from your topic. You can use more lines if necessary.

- On each line that comes from a thick line, write further ideas that come from those words and phrases.

- If you want, you can expand the diagram to write more related ideas by writing on the dotted lines.

Remember that the most important task of brainstorming is to get as many ideas about your topic as possible.

Step 3: Organizing

Take the ideas in your circle diagram and organize them by making an outline for each body paragraph similar to the one on page 7.

- Write your thesis statement. You can use one from Practice 6 if you like.

- Make the topic on each thick line above a topic sentence for a paragraph.

- The information on the thin and dotted lines could become the major and minor supports for each body paragraph.

Remember that this is just a step in the process. As you make your outline, you may delete some ideas that are not relevant to the paragraph and/or include additional points.

Step 4: Writing the First Draft

Many writers find it useful to write the thesis statement first, add the body paragraphs, and then write the introductory and concluding paragraphs. Some writers type their essays and save them so that further drafts are easier to change. Other writers prefer to write their first draft by hand. You need to find out which method works best for you.

Note: At this point in the writing process, you should walk away from your essay for at least an hour or even a day. By doing this, you can read your essay with a "fresh" eye.

Step 5: Rewriting

Read your essay again and look carefully at the content and the organization. Mark any changes that you want to make. Then look for problems in grammar and punctuation. Use the Peer Help Worksheet on page 20 to help you focus your attention on points for revision and editing.

Before writing your final draft, you may find it helpful to repeat Steps 4 and 5.

Step 6: Writing the Final Draft

Write your final draft. Be sure to use acceptable essay format. See Appendix 1 on page 163.

Peer Help Worksheet

Trade essays and textbooks with a classmate. Read your classmate's essay while your classmate reads yours. Check off (✓) the items in your partner's book as you evaluate them. Then return the essays and books. If any of the items in your book are not checked off, and you agree with your partner, correct your essay before turning it in. Use a pencil if you write on your classmate's essay or book.

CONTENT

1 Is the thesis statement presented clearly? . . . . ❑

2 Do all the body paragraphs support the thesis statement? . . . . . ❑

ORGANIZATION

1 Circle the thesis statement. Underline the controlling idea. Put a box around the predictor, if any.

2 Are the body paragraphs well organized? . . . . ❑

    a. Do they have topic sentences? . . . . ❑

    b. Do they have concluding sentences? . . . . ❑

    c. Do they use bridges? . . . . ❑

3 What elements does the concluding paragraph have? (Check all that apply.)

    a. summary . . . . ❑

    b. restatement of the thesis statement . . . . ❑

    c. final comment . . . . ❑

LANGUAGE

1 Has the writer avoided using choppy sentences? . . . . ❑

    If not, point out any possible problem areas to the writer.

2 Do you think commas and semicolons are used correctly? . . . . . ❑

    If not, discuss any possible mistakes with the writer.

Writing to Communicate . . . More

Choose one of the topics below to write about in a journal or for an in-class essay. You can choose to focus on writing fluently, or you can practice any of the organizational techniques, sentence patterns, or language points discussed in this chapter.

1. Should arts education be required in public schools? Why or why not?

2. Would you rather read a book or see a movie? Why?

3. Do you know any artistic or creative people? What do they do?

4. Many entertainers earn very high salaries. Do you approve or disapprove of this? Why?

THE CAUSE AND EFFECT ESSAY

Language and Communication

I WRITING FOCUS

Cause and Effect

A common approach to academic writing is to **analyze** a topic by taking it apart and examining each part. One way to do this is to look at the **causes** and **effects** of a situation. In other words, you analyze the reasons and examine the results. For example, you may analyze an event in history by discussing what led to the event and then describing what the result of the event was.

■ PRACTICE 1: Identifying Causes and Effects

*Work with a classmate. For each topic, write **C** if the item below is a cause, **E** if it is an effect, **CE** if it is both, and **X** if it is neither. Discuss your choices.*

1. miscommunication

   _____ speaking a different language   _____ losing a job

   _____ not hearing   _____ sending an e-mail

   _____ not paying attention   _____ feeling embarrassed

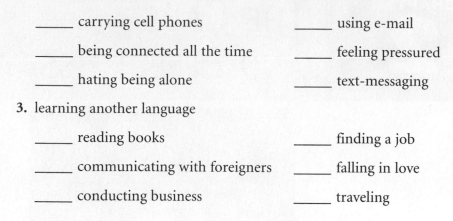

2. fast communication

_____ carrying cell phones	_____ using e-mail
_____ being connected all the time	_____ feeling pressured
_____ hating being alone	_____ text-messaging

3. learning another language

_____ reading books	_____ finding a job
_____ communicating with foreigners	_____ falling in love
_____ conducting business	_____ traveling

Problems of Oversimplification and Correlation

Discussing causes and effects can be problematic because few events can be traced to a single cause or have only one effect. One problem is **oversimplification**, or incorrectly assuming that only one event directly caused another. For example:

➤ The cause of the accident was the heavy traffic.

Heavy traffic alone cannot cause an accident. Something else has to occur (e.g., rainy weather, faulty brakes, sleepy driver). The writer here is oversimplifying the reasons for the accident. A more accurate statement would be:

➤ One cause of the accident was the heavy traffic.

Another common problem in assessing the cause of something is confusion between **correlation** and **causation**. You should not assume that because two events are correlated (i.e., close to each other in space or time) that one event caused the other. For example:

➤ I saw Jane walk by your house just before your car was stolen. Jane must have stolen your car.

There is no reason to think that Jane had anything to do with the stolen car simply because she happened to be in the area when the car was stolen.

■ PRACTICE 2: Determining True Cause and Effect Relationships

Read each situation below with a classmate. Determine the cause and the effect. Then decide whether the cause and effect relationship is valid.

1. If they have enough sunlight and water, most plants will grow.

2. Wayne must have learned Japanese because he spent three years living in Japan.

3. The French midterm exam was too hard. As a result, I failed it.

4. The mayor stole money from the city and left the country. Because of this, there is no money for language classes at the elementary school.

5. The Icelandic language hasn't changed much, so children there can read ancient texts.

6. I assume that Nadia speaks Russian since both of her parents do.

Writing an Essay Outline

Good essay writers study the characteristics of organization to learn how to write, but they also learn by reading other essays. In other essays, they can see not only the fundamental basics of essay writing but also the many variations on those basics. Then they can pattern their own writing on what they have read.

As discussed in Chapter 1, outlining is a good way to understand the organization of a piece of writing as well as a good way to organize your own writing. When you outline an essay while reading it, you learn how to outline and organize your own essays. Your outlines can be very simple, with just one or two words for each paragraph, or they can be more detailed with information about topic sentences and supporting sentences.

Most cause and effect essays follow one of two basic organizational patterns. The first discusses all the causes and/or effects separately in "blocks." A block can be one or more paragraphs. The block style has two common variations. In one you discuss both causes and effects, and in the other you discuss only causes or only effects. In the second basic pattern, you have a series of one-cause/one-effect paragraphs, where each cause is "linked" to one effect. The simple outlines below show these patterns.

Block Pattern 1	**Block Pattern 2**	**Linking Pattern**
I. Introduction	I. Introduction	I. Introduction
II. Causes	II. Cause *or* Effect	II. Cause → Effect
III. Effects	III. Cause *or* Effect	III. Cause → Effect
IV. Conclusion	IV. Cause *or* Effect	IV. Cause → Effect
	V. Conclusion	V. Conclusion

■ PRACTICE 3: Outlining an Essay

As you read Model Essay 1, complete the outline on page 25. Which pattern does this essay represent?

Model Essay 1

Changes in the English Language

That English, like all languages, has changed over the years is clear to any student of English literature who tries to read Chaucer[1]. The English that he wrote in the twelfth century is nearly unintelligible today. Unfortunately, this is the first effect of language change: a barrier[2] to understanding. *Why* languages change is another topic—one that can be analyzed. In general, linguists agree that there are two basic causes of language change: simplification and contact with other languages.

Over time, speakers simplify a language by making it more efficient. The pronunciation of English, for example, has undergone change in order to make it easier. For example, researchers have determined that words in Old English were spoken almost exactly as they were written. Because of this, we know that in Old English,

(continued)

the "gh" in *bought* was pronounced. However, pronouncing the *gh* before the *t* is not an efficient use of the mouth, so in Modern English, the *gh* is silent. Anyone who has tried to figure out the spelling system of English knows that there are many words with silent letters: *debt, know, honor, autumn, business, whole, build.*

Another way of simplifying a language also leads to change. Speakers often make analogies between grammatical structures within the language in order to regularize them. For example, many irregular verbs in English have changed due to the desire to simplify. The changes are made by making an analogy between regular verbs and irregular verbs. The past tense of such irregular verbs as *burn* and *dream* used to be *burnt* and *dreamt*, but they have regularized to *burned* and *dreamed*. In short, one major cause of language change is the desire of speakers to simplify it.

The second major cause of language change happens when speakers of different languages come in contact. This is particularly true with vocabulary. Everyone can recognize common cognates[3], such as *hospital* from the French *hôpital*. However, few speakers of English know that such everyday words as *banana, chocolate, hey, ketchup,* and *magazine* come from such diverse languages as Wolof (West Africa), Nahuatl (Central Mexico), Norwegian, Chinese, and Arabic, respectively. In fact, nearly one third of all English words can trace their origin back to French. This is because, in 1066, the Normans of present-day France conquered England and became the ruling class for 300 years. There are even leftover structures of French grammar in English.

For example, in English, adjectives come before nouns, but in French, adjectives come after nouns. There are set phrases in English, however, that still have the adjective after the noun: *president elect, surgeon general, times past*, and *stage left*. These phrases don't change; that is, the combination of noun and adjective isn't separated. However, there are a few adjectives, such as *proper* and *aplenty,* which are used more freely. For example, speakers can say that they live in *New York proper* or *San Francisco proper*, and that they have *apples aplenty* or *friends aplenty.*

In short, English, like other languages, is always changing. Speakers attempt to simplify the pronunciation and grammar to make them more efficient. When English speakers come in contact with speakers of languages, both languages will influence each other by adopting vocabulary and even some grammatical structures. For linguists, these changes are the heart of their research, but for an everyday speaker of a language, the changes can also be of interest. You are living during a time of changes in your language. Can you spot any?

[1]**Chaucer** *proper n.* Geoffrey Chaucer (?1340–1400), an English writer known for his long poem *The Canterbury Tales*, one of the most important works in English literature

[2]**barrier** *n.* something that prevents people from doing something

[3]**cognate** *n.* a word that has a similar meaning and spelling in two languages, such as *address* (English) and *Adresse* (German)

I. Introductory paragraph
   A. Hook
      1. _____
      2. Transition to causes of language change
   B. Thesis statement
      1. Two basic causes of language change
         a) _____
         b) Contact with other languages

II. Simplify by making language more efficient
   A. _____
      1. _____
      2. _____
   B. Bridge to next paragraph
      1. Analogies between grammatical structure to regularize
         a) _____
         b) _____
   C. Concluding sentence

III. _____
   A. _____
      1. Examples: banana, chocolate, hey, ketchup, magazine
      2. _____
   B. Bridge to next paragraph
   C. Some N ADJ in English
      1. Static phrases that don't change
      2. _____

IV. Concluding paragraph
   A. Restatement of thesis
   B. Final comment

■ PRACTICE 4: **Reorganizing an Essay**

Complete the outline of Model Essay 2, which is organized according to the Block Pattern 2. Then, using the same information, complete the Linking Pattern outline.

Model Essay 2

Nonverbal Miscommunication

Misunderstandings between people happen for many reasons. This can be especially true when two people have different language and cultural backgrounds. It's clear how people who don't speak the same language can be misunderstood, but understanding what people are saying when they aren't speaking can be equally

(continued)

problematic. Cultural differences in nonverbal communication can cause considerable cultural misunderstandings.

Nonverbal signals are learned at a very young age by observing the people in your culture. Eye contact is very culturally dependent. In some cultures, making eye contact is essential to communication, while in other cultures, it is a sign of disrespect. The distance that people stand apart from each other is also culturally determined. In addition, what you do with your hands and how you gesture with them are culturally bound forms of communication. The effects of these cultural differences do not cause misunderstandings with people with similar cultural backgrounds, but they can lead to comical as well as serious misunderstanding between people raised in different cultures.

For example, in North American cultures, it is usual for people to look each other in the eye when they are talking. If one person doesn't, the other person may think that the first person is lying or being evasive[1]. However, in many Asian cultures, it is considered impolite to look someone in the eye, especially in the workplace with people in a higher position. This simple difference can lead to direct misunderstanding between people from these countries. The North Americans will probably think that the Asians are hiding something, and the Asians will probably think that the North Americans are being rude.

In the United States, it is common for people of European descent[2] to stand about eighteen inches, or the length of an arm, apart when they are having a conversation. On the other hand, people of Central and South American heritage stand much closer to each other—about a foot closer. This difference can cause a "dance" in which the European American keeps backing up to maintain an eighteen-inch separation, while the Latino keeps stepping closer to narrow the gap. The result is that the Latino may think that the European American is trying to avoid him or her. On the other hand, the European American may think that the Latino is sending a romantic message since being closer than a foot is a sign of intimacy[3] in the European American's mind.

A difference in meaning with one gesture can cause a somewhat comical misunderstanding. In the United States, people wave goodbye to each other by lifting their arm and, with the palm of the hand facing out, moving the hand up and down or back and forth. However, a very similar gesture means

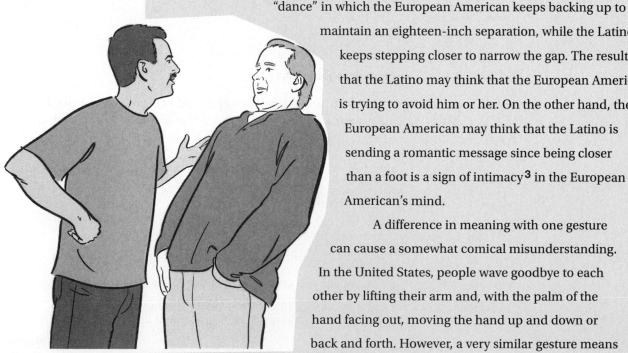

What about you?

What are the customs about eye contact in your culture? Tell a classmate.

"come here" in many Asian countries. Therefore, just as the Asian is asking the North American to come closer to him or her, the North American is waving goodbye and going in the opposite direction.

In conclusion, when you are interacting with people of different cultures, it's a good idea to learn how they communicate—both verbally and nonverbally. Not understanding the customs of eye contact, personal space, and gestures can cause a lot of miscommunication—both comical and serious.

[1]**evasive** *adj.* not willing to answer questions directly

[2]**descent** *n.* your family origins, especially in relation to the country where your family came from

[3]**intimacy** *n.* a state of having a close, personal relationship with someone

Block Pattern 2

I. Introduction
II. Cultural differences
   A. _____
   B. _____
   C. Gestures
III. Effects of differences in eye contact
IV. _____
V. _____
VI. Conclusion

Linking Pattern

I. Introduction
II. _____
   A. North American
   B. Asian
III. Cultural differences lead to misunderstandings due to differences in personal space
   A. _____
   B. _____
IV. _____
   A. _____
   B. _____
V. Conclusion

Introductory Paragraphs

As you learned in Chapter 1, an essay begins with an introductory paragraph, which ends with the thesis statement. What comes before the thesis statement must "hook" the reader; that is, it must make the reader want to read your essay. In addition, the transition from the hook to the thesis statement must be clear. Sometimes the transition is just a word, and sometimes it is a sentence. There are several ways to hook the reader.

Cause and Effect Hooks

In an essay that discusses the causes only, a good introductory paragraph may briefly mention the **effects**. Similarly, in an essay only about the effects of something, your introductory paragraph could briefly mention the **causes**. In this introductory paragraph from Model Essay 1, the mention of an effect of language change leads to the thesis statement about the causes of language change.

Model Introductory Paragraph 1

Effects of Languages not Changing	That English, like all languages, has changed over the years is clear to any student of English literature who tries to read Chaucer. The English that he wrote in the twelfth century is nearly unintelligible today. Unfortunately, this is the first effect of language change: a barrier to understanding.
Connecting Sentence	*Why* languages change is another topic—one that can be analyzed.
Thesis Statement	In general, linguists agree that there are two basic causes of language change: simplification for efficiency or regularity and contact with other languages.

General-to-Specific Hooks

A common hook begins with a **general point** and narrows it down to a **specific point**, which is your thesis statement. In this introductory paragraph from Model Essay 2, the topic of "misunderstandings" starts very broad and narrows to the thesis statement.

Model Introductory Paragraph 2

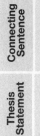

General Point: Misunderstandings between people happen for many reasons. This can be especially true when two people are from different language and cultural backgrounds.

Connecting Sentence: It is clear how people who don't speak the same language can be misunderstood, but understanding what people are saying when they aren't speaking can be equally problematic.

Thesis Statement: Cultural differences in nonverbal communication can cause considerable cultural misunderstandings.

Personal Anecdote Hooks

Another way of introducing your thesis statement is to write a **personal anecdote**, or story, about an event that is relevant to the topic. Model 3 is this type of hook.

Model Introductory Paragraph 3

Personal Anecdote	I have lived in the United States for over 20 years now. I moved here in my early twenties, alone and without my family, in order to attend college. As so often happens, I met a man, fell in love, and married him. I travel home as often as possible, but the time between visits is getting longer and longer. Even though I can still speak my native language, I find it increasingly difficult to remember words. In fact, I find it easier to use English, and my relatives back home are happy to use English with me since they want to practice. As the years go by, I feel more at ease in English.
Connecting Sentence	This upsets and surprises me.
Thesis Statement	People can lose comfort in their own native languages in several different ways.

Historical Hooks

Another type of hook gives a **historical perspective** on your topic. In this type of hook, you write about an event in history that relates to your topic. Model 4 discusses the historical context in which the English language changed, which is the topic of Model Essay 1.

Model Introductory Paragraph 4

Historical Background	In 1066, the Duke of Normandy, also known as William the Conqueror, succeeded in defeating the English armies, which marked the beginning of profound changes in English rule. England became less influenced by Scandinavia and closer to the countries of the European continent. 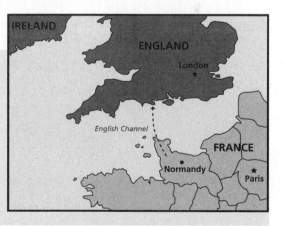
Connecting Sentence	This influence penetrated all parts of life, including culture and commerce.
Thesis Statement	The English language as well underwent many changes during this period.

■ **PRACTICE 5: Writing Introductory Paragraphs**

In Practice 1 on pages 21–22, you determined some causes and effects for three topics. Choose one of those topics and write a thesis statement. Then write two different types of introductory paragraphs for the thesis statement.

II SENTENCE FOCUS

Avoiding Stringy Sentences

In Chapter 1, you learned to avoid choppy sentences by combining them into longer sentences. If you combine too many independent clauses, however, you may end up with a **stringy sentence**. A stringy sentence has too many independent clauses, perhaps through an overuse of coordinating conjunctions or subordinating conjunctions. For example:

➤ When you study a language, you learn another way of communicating,
        1st clause   2nd clause

    but you must also study the culture because you need to know the
      3rd   4th

    context in which the language is spoken because, if you don't, you can still
                5th   6th   7th

    be misunderstood even though you may speak the language perfectly.
                                8th

One way to make this sentence less stringy is to divide it into two sentences by using a transition instead of a coordinating conjunction. Here is a list of the transitions that mean the same as the coordinating conjunctions:

Coordinating Conjunction	Transition
and	moreover in addition
but yet	however on the other hand
so	therefore as a result

Here is the stringy sentence divided into two sentences by using a transition instead of the coordinating conjunction:

➤ When you study a language, you learn another way of communicating.
        1st clause   2nd

    However, you must also study the culture because you need to know the
              1st clause   2nd

    context in which the language is spoken because, if you don't, you can still
                3rd   4th   5th

    be misunderstood even though you may speak the language perfectly.
                                6th

This is now less stringy, but it still needs work. The second sentence has six clauses—one independent clause, one adjective clause, and four adverbial clauses. By changing an adverbial clause into a separate sentence, you can make the sentence less stringy still. Below is a list of subordinating conjunctions and the transitions that have similar meanings:

Subordinating Conjunction	Transition
after	after that next
before	before that previously
while	meanwhile
even though although	nevertheless nonetheless
whereas while	on the other hand in contrast
if	otherwise

Here is the stringy sentence now divided into three sentences. Since it is no longer stringy, it is easier to understand.

➤ When you study a language, you learn another way of communicating.
   1st clause   2nd

However, you must also study the culture because you need to know the
     1st clause   2nd

context in which the language is spoken. Otherwise, you can still be
     3rd   1st clause

misunderstood even though you may speak the language perfectly.
         2nd

■ PRACTICE 6: Rewriting Stringy Sentences

Work with a classmate and rewrite each of the following sentences to make them less stringy.

1. When I moved to a small village in Croatia, I didn't speak the language, so it was hard for me to talk with people because most Croatians at that time didn't speak English, but I found a tutor, and I learned Croatian, so by the time I left Croatia ten months later, I spoke the language fairly well.

2. Snapping your fingers to get someone's attention is a common gesture in many countries, but in the United States it is considered a very rude way to get someone's attention, so this gesture should be avoided when you travel to the United States.

3. Since English has many French and German words, there are many false cognates, so French and German speaking learners of English have to be careful when they use English because they may be misunderstood.

4. Blanche's mother is French, and her father is Turkish, so she learned both languages when she was growing up although she mostly speaks English now because she is married to a Canadian.

5. When I was visiting Kiri today, her mother, who doesn't speak English, wanted me to see a painting in her room, so she gestured to me to follow her, but I misunderstood and thought that she wanted me to leave, so I started waving goodbye while she kept gesturing to me to follow her.

III LANGUAGE FOCUS

Collocations

Collocations are two or more words that commonly go together. Collocations are common in academic writing, and using them correctly can add to the sophistication of your writing. Study the sentences below that use common collocations for cause and effect.

Phrasal Verb Collocations

➤ The Norman invasion **brought about** a change in English vocabulary.

➤ Contact with other languages **brings forth** changes in vocabulary.

➤ The desire for easy pronunciation in the past **gave rise to** very difficult spelling nowadays.

➤ Speaking a new language **leads to** better fluency.

➤ Spelling changes often **result from** a desire for greater simplicity.

Adjective and Noun Collocations

➤ The **immediate cause** of the death of the Yana language was the death of its last native speaker.

➤ The **underlying cause** was the near total destruction of the Yana people by the European settlers in California.

➤ A **likely cause** of frustration when speaking your native language is not remembering words.

➤ An **unlikely cause** is that you're forgetting your native language.

➤ Spending a year in Chile had the **desired effect**. I learned Spanish.

➤ We may never know the **full effect** of losing so many languages.

➤ The speaker's accent had a **modest effect** on the audience's understanding of his lecture.

Idiom Collocations

➤ Students often **feel the effects of** learning a second language most at the end of the day when their brains can't think in any language!

➤ You may **suffer the consequences of** not studying your vocabulary.

➤ Our lack of understanding of common nonverbal gestures **set the foundation for** our total frustration.

■ PRACTICE 7: Using Collocations

Fill in each blank with one of the collocations given in the box above the paragraph. There are two extra collocations in each box. You can use each collocation only once.

resulted from	gave rise to
the desired effect	the immediate cause
feel the effects of	a modest effect

1. Hawaiian Pidgin, spoken in the Hawaiian islands, first _____ language contact among English settlers and the native Hawaiian people. Then, in the 1800s, immigrants from China, Japan, Korea, Portugal, and the Philippines came to Hawaii to work on the sugar plantations. Obviously, the workers needed to communicate with each other and the English and Hawaiian-speaking plantation owners, and this need _____ another form of Pidgin. The new language had _____; workers and owners were able to communicate. Linguistically, the other languages had _____ on English grammar; the grammar of Pidgin is actually quite close to that of English. They had a larger effect on vocabulary, with such words as *pau* for *finished*, from Hawaiian, and *akamai* for *smart*, from Japanese. Some expressions are reductions of English words, such as *brah* (brother) and *howzit?* (How's it going?). When you visit Hawaii, keep your ears open for Pidgin and see if you can understand it. Then try to learn some yourself!

a modest effect	set the foundation for
bring forth	the full effect of
led to	the underlying cause of

2. _____ the renaissance of the Welsh language is the fact the Welsh people didn't want their language to die out. This desire _____ many parents speaking Welsh to their children at home. The determination of the Welsh people also _____ Welsh schools, a new Welsh publishing industry, and a lot more people speaking Welsh in the streets of such Welsh cities as Cardiff and Bangor. No doubt, _____ the rebirth of this beloved language is still to come.

IV Writing to Communicate

Your Turn

Choose one of the topics below, and write a cause and/or effect essay. Follow the steps of the writing process (analyzing the topic, brainstorming, organizing, writing the first draft, rewriting, writing the final draft).

1. Review the three aspects of nonverbal communication that were discussed in Model Essay 1 in terms of your culture. Then give some personal examples of the effects of misunderstandings based on those aspects.

2. What are the effects of our increasing use of written communication, such as e-mail, instant messaging, or phone text messaging, on communication?

3. Have you ever studied another language? Why did you decide to learn another language? How has your life changed because of it?

Peer Help Worksheet

Trade essays and textbooks with a classmate. Read your classmate's essay while your classmate reads yours. Check off (✓) the items in your partner's book as you evaluate them. Then return the essays and books. If any of the items in your book are not checked off, and you agree with your partner, correct your essay before turning it in. Use a pencil if you write on your classmate's essay or book.

CONTENT

1 Is the topic appropriate for a cause and effect essay? . . . . ❏

2 Are the causes and effects clearly explained? . . . . ❏

ORGANIZATION

1 Does the introductory paragraph grab the reader's attention? . . . ❏

What does the hook do? (Check one.)

   a. Discusses causes or effects . . . . ❏

   b. Starts with general information and leads to the specific thesis statement . . . . ❏

   c. Gives a personal anecdote . . . . ❏

   d. Gives a historical perspective . . . . ❏

2 Circle the thesis statement. Underline the controlling idea.

Put a box around the predictor, if any.

3 Are the body paragraphs well organized? . . . . ❏

   a. Do they have topic sentences? . . . . ❏

   b. Do they have concluding sentences? . . . . ❏

   c. Do they use bridges? . . . . ❏

4 What elements of concluding paragraphs does the concluding paragraph in this essay have? (Check all that apply.)

   a. summary . . . . ❏

   b. restatement of the thesis statement . . . . ❏

   c. final comment . . . . ❏

LANGUAGE

1 Has the writer avoided using stringy sentences? . . . . ❏

2 Are commas and semicolons used correctly? . . . . ❏

If not, discuss any possible mistakes with the writer.

Writing to Communicate . . . More

As a journal entry or an in-class timed essay, choose one of the topics below. You can choose to focus on writing fluently, or you can practice any of the organizational techniques, sentence patterns, or language points discussed in this chapter.

1. Analyze the causes and/or effects on language since the beginning of the electronic age.
2. Discuss some of the nonverbal miscommunications you have had with people from other cultures. Analyze the causes and effects of each.
3. How has globalization affected language?

THE PROBLEM AND SOLUTION ESSAY

Campus Life

I WRITING FOCUS

Problem and Solution

Many successful academic essays start with students taking a stand on an issue and then explaining the validity of their position. This is especially true for **problem and solution** essays, in which the writers must convince the readers that their solution to a particular problem makes sense and will work. This type of essay is common in many fields of study, including business, political science, economics, and law.

The organization of a problem and solution essay has the same overall structure as other essays, but the content of each paragraph is more firmly set in the following pattern.

- The introductory paragraph starts with a **description of a problem** as the "hook" and ends with the **proposed solution**, which is the thesis statement.

- The first body paragraph discusses the **benefits** to implementing the proposed solution.

- The next body paragraph(s) discuss any **objections** that you think a reader would have to your proposal and the **counter-objections**. The counter-objections explain why the objections aren't really problems. Each counter-objection is directly related to an objection. Three styles you can use to present this part of the essay are diagrammed on the next page.

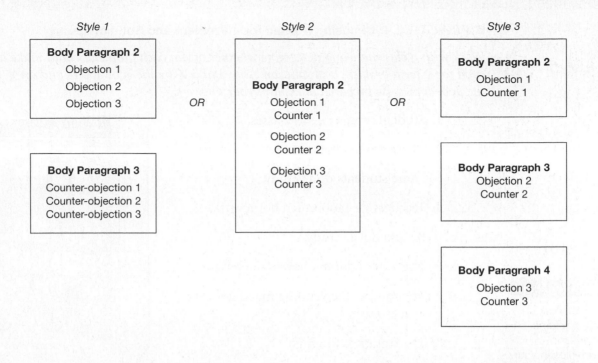

- The concluding paragraph ends the essay with a strong **restatement** of the proposed solution, a **summary** of the major benefits, and a **call to action** or **final comment**. A call to action asks your reader to do something in support of the proposed solution, such as change habits or write a letter. This isn't always applicable to a topic, so you may choose to write a final comment instead.

Guidelines for Choosing a Topic

Be sure that the problem can be solved and that the solution you propose is workable.

Problem: Books for students are too expensive.

Solution: Schools should purchase books for each class for students to use and return at the end of the course.

1. Avoid choosing an insignificant problem.

Problem: There isn't enough chalk for the chalkboard.

2. Avoid problems that do not have solutions.

Problem: There is too much hate in the world.

Solution: ?

3. Avoid solutions that are not practical.

Problem: When students go far away to school, they get lonely.

Solution: Students should make friends quickly.

A better solution to this problem would be:

Solution: Students who are lonely should join study groups and clubs to meet other students who may become friends.

■ PRACTICE 1: Choosing a Topic for a Problem and Solution Essay

Work with a classmate and determine whether or not each problem would make a good topic for a problem and solution essay. Put a ✓ by the good topics and an ✗ by the poor topics. Be prepared to explain your answers.

_____ 1. Students come late to classes.

_____ 2. There are too many students in classes.

_____ 3. Some students don't study.

_____ 4. Teachers give too much homework.

_____ 5. It's too hot to study.

_____ 6. The school doesn't have a cafeteria.

_____ 7. The food in the vending machines isn't always fresh.

_____ 8. The tuition is too high.

_____ 9. The cafeteria food is unhealthy.

_____ 10. The school doesn't have a business department.

> **What about you?**
>
> Can you think of other problems that arise in universities in your country? Share your thoughts with a classmate.

■ PRACTICE 2: Finding Solutions to Problems

Work with a classmate. Choose three of the acceptable problems presented in Practice 1 and write a solution to each.

1. Problem number: _____
   Possible solution: _____

   _____

2. Problem number: _____
   Possible solution: _____

   _____

3. Problem number: _____
   Possible solution: _____

   _____

Objections and Counter-Objections

For a problem and solution essay to be convincing, it is necessary to anticipate the objections that a reader may have to your solution. Then, counter those objections by indicating that they aren't significant or that they can easily be overcome. For each objection, there must be a clear counter-objection. For example:

Problem:	The campus is so large that it's difficult to get to from one class to another in time.
Solution:	The school should provide more time between classes.
Objection:	Providing more time will cut time from classes.
Counter:	To make up the difference, the school day will start earlier and end later.

■ PRACTICE 3: Determining Objections and Counter-Objections

For each problem and solution below, write in an objection and a counter-objection. Work with a classmate.

1. Problem: Classes are too crowded.
   Solution: The school should hire more teachers.
   Objection: _____

   _____

   Counter: _____

   _____

2. Problem: Housing is difficult for students to find.
   Solution: The school should provide a bulletin board where housing
                messages can be posted.
   Objection: _____

   _____

   Counter: _____

   _____

3. Problem: Some students want more homework; others don't want any.
   Solution: Teachers should give a minimum and a maximum amount of
                homework.
   Objection: _____

   _____

   Counter: _____

   _____

■ PRACTICE 4: Analyzing the Model Essays

With a classmate, discuss these questions about each of the Model Essays on pages 40–43.

1. What problem is described in the introductory paragraph?

2. What is the proposed solution?

3. How many benefits to the proposal are listed in the first body paragraph? What are they?

4. List the objections and counter-objections of each essay.

   a. How many objections are there in each? Circle the language used to signal the objections.

   b. Are each of these objections addressed? Circle the language used to signal the counter-objections.

   c. How does the organization of Model Essay 1 differ from Model Essay 2?

   d. Does the concluding paragraph have a call to action, a final comment, or both?

Getting to Class on Time

Professors who have early morning classes often encounter the problem of students coming late to class. Sometimes, there may be only two or three students in the class on time. This makes it difficult for professors to begin their classes. They want to start for the students who are there on time, but they know if they do, the latecomers will miss the beginning of the lesson, and the professor will have to catch them up later. For the sake of the on-time students and the professor, there need to be consequences for the students who regularly arrive late. Therefore, a late policy in which attendance is made part of the final class grade and late students are marked absent for every three times they are late should be implemented.

There are several benefits to establishing this policy. First of all, if students know that there are negative consequences to being late, they will try harder to be on time. Therefore, more students will be in attendance when the professor is ready to start class. In addition, no matter how quietly a late student enters the class, it always disturbs the class, so this late policy means that there will be fewer interruptions to the class by students coming in late. Most importantly, students will be there from the beginning and will not have to figure out what the professor is talking about or what the other students are working on, which can happen when they arrive late.

Some people may object to this solution on the grounds that it is punitive[1] in nature and treats students like children. They may ask why students should be punished for arriving late a few times. However, this policy does not affect those students who are late a few times. In fact, there are no consequences for being late once or twice. The consequences begin when students are late three or more times. For there truly to be a noticeable effect on a student's grade, he or she would have to be late once or twice a week.

Another objection that some students may have is that the point of the class is for them to learn. If they can get an A on a test or a paper, there is no reason for them to even attend the class, much less be there on time. However, the truth is that in universities in the United States, a lot of learning *does* happen in class. In fact, it is often impossible to pass a class without understanding a professor's lecture since what the professor is lecturing about is not in a textbook. Also, a student cannot demonstrate proficiency in a language class, for example, without attending the class. When students are chronically[2] late, they not only miss a lot of learning, but they disturb the other students who are trying to learn.

A final objection may concern the inequality of the policy with regards to other classes and universities. The point of this objection is that since most classes in universities do not have a late policy, none of them should. This is a mistake in reasoning. To say that one class should have or not have a policy because all the other classes have or don't have it negates the individuality of classes and professors. For instance, a biology lecture class with five hundred students has different needs than a Spanish literature class with fifteen students. Each class needs a different policy.

In conclusion, the problem of getting students to come on time to early morning classes can be greatly reduced if a late policy is initiated by the professor. It will give those students who are habitually late a gentle push to be on time, and more importantly, it will give both the professor and those students who are on time a period of uninterrupted class time.

What about you?

What is the policy about being late to class in your country? Is it acceptable? Is it allowed? Share your answer with a classmate.

[1]**punitive** *adj.* designed to punish someone

[2]**chronically** *adv.* when something happens for a long time and cannot be stopped

Model Essay 2

The Buddy[1] System

As an undergraduate science professor in a large university, I see students from all around the world in my classes. I've noticed that most of the foreign students stick with[2] other students from their countries, and few make friends with the American students in my classes. However, when I talk to my students individually, the majority of both foreign students and American students say that they would like to get to know each other. Therefore, I've established a "buddy" system in my classes in which I pair up each foreign student with an American or sometimes two. I propose that this system be adopted university-wide.

There are many benefits to this program, the most obvious of which is the cross-cultural experience that both students have. I match the American students with someone from a country that they are interested in. Since the foreign students are already here, I assume that they want to be paired up with an American student, but I have had a few cases where two foreign students from different countries wanted to be paired up. Another benefit is the trade of information that happens. The foreign student learns the ins and outs[3] of life on a university campus in the United States, and the American student may in turn get help with the science that I teach. The biggest benefit is that sometimes lifelong friendships are formed. I believe that these types of friendships are the ones that will keep us all working for world peace.

Of course, some of my colleagues will object to my buddy student program. Some will say that they don't want to force students to become friends with someone. Others will say that it's a waste of class time and that it's my job to teach science, not to facilitate[4] friendships. Still others will object on the basis that some students may take advantage of their buddy in any number of ways.

To my colleagues who have objections to this program because they don't want to require students to become friends, I can explain that the program is completely voluntary. I don't force any student to participate, but I can say with certainty that a large majority always choose to participate. I also maintain that it is not a waste of class time and certainly not of my time. In fact, the buddies save me time by answering for each other the questions they might ask of me. Besides, of the 54 hours I have to teach my semester-long course, I can spare[5] a half hour to match students with each other. Finally, our university students might be taken advantage of or hurt by other students regardless of what professors do. It will not be more or less likely to happen in the buddy system.

In conclusion, I strongly urge my colleagues to adopt the buddy system in their undergraduate lecture classes. It can enrich both foreign and American students by gaining an appreciation of another culture, by trading information, and by establishing long-lasting friendships.

What about you?

Are you interested in meeting other students in your classes who have different backgrounds from yours? Would you appreciate a program like the one described in the essay? Share your thoughts with a classmate.

[1]**buddy** *n*. a friend
[2]**stick with** *v*. to stay together
[3]**ins and outs** *n*. all of the details of something, such as a system or a profession

[4]**facilitate** *v*. to make it easier for a process or activity to happen

[5]**spare** *v*. to give because it's extra for you

Paragraph Unity

One of the most important characteristics in writing in English is **paragraph unity**. A paragraph has unity when all the supporting sentences are relevant to the topic sentence. A sentence that does not support the topic sentence is called an **irrelevant sentence** and should be eliminated. Look at the sample paragraph on page 43. It has one sentence that does not belong in it because it does not support the topic sentence about the writer's first day on campus. Cross the irrelevant sentence out.

Sample Paragraph

My First Day on Campus

My first day on my new campus was very exciting. I arrived early and found where my dorm room was. I met my roommate for the first time, and I knew instantly that we would get along well. Her name is Ayla, and she is from Turkey. I've never met anyone from Turkey before! After we unpacked our clothes, Ayla and I went to the cafeteria for lunch. After lunch, we went to a "mixer" where we met other new students. There were also speakers who told us about living on campus. After dinner in the cafeteria, a free movie with popcorn was shown. After it ended, Ayla and I went back to our dorm room, where we talked until 2 A.M. All in all, my first day in my new home was great.

The sentence that you should have crossed out is, "I've never met anyone from Turkey before!" This sentence is irrelevant because it does not support the topic sentence by discussing the activities of the writer's first day on campus.

■ **PRACTICE 5: Finding Irrelevant Sentences**

Read each paragraph below. Cross out any irrelevant sentences that you find. Note that there may be more than one irrelevant sentence in a paragraph, or there may not be any. Discuss your answers with a classmate.

1.
Living in a Dorm

When students go to college in a town far away from their hometown, they find they are totally responsible for themselves for perhaps the first time in their lives. There are no curfews, so they may decide to stay out all night. There is no one telling them to study, so they may fail classes. There is no one to cook for them, so they may eat at fast food restaurants all the time. In fact, many freshmen are not used to organizing their time or making decisions by themselves. For all of these reasons, it should be mandatory for first-year students to live in dorms.

2.
Community Colleges

Attending a community college (a two-year college) can be a very wise way to start your higher education. There are over 1,600 community colleges in the United States. Usually, community colleges offer the same classes as universities do in their first two years of study. These classes are basic education classes that students need to take before they can take classes in their major. In addition, in a community college, these classes are taught by professors because the main duty of a professor there is to teach students. In many universities, professors mostly do research, and the lower division classes are taught by graduate students. Finally, community college tuition is much less than a university's. The average tuition for a year at a community college is $2,500. In contrast, the average university tuition for a year is more than twice that. In fact, when I went to a university, my tuition for my first year was $10,000 dollars, and this was a public school! In short, there are many benefits to going to a community college.

3.
Succeeding in a University Class

Participating in class discussions can be scary, but following certain suggestions can make it easier. The reason to participate is so the professor will get to know you and, when the time comes, write a good letter of recommendation for you. First of all, try to say something the first or second day of class even if it is to ask a simple question about the syllabus. The longer you wait to make your first comment, the more difficult it becomes. Second, take notes during a class discussion. This will help you pay attention and follow the progression of the discussion. You can even write down questions you may have and ask them later. Third, when you are ready to say something, lean forward in your chair and raise your finger or pencil a little. Relate your comment or question to what someone else said. Finally, remember that it is not enough to say something one time in one class. You must continue to participate the whole term. You'll be surprised that participating may become easy. In short, by making an effort, you can be a successful participant in your university class.

Avoiding Run-on Sentences and Comma Splices

You have learned how to avoid choppy and stringy sentences by correctly using sentence connectors (i.e., transitions, coordinating conjunctions, and subordinating conjunctions). When you revise these sentences, you need to punctuate the beginnings and endings of sentences correctly to avoid **run-on sentences**. Run-on sentences occur when two or more sentences are punctuated as one sentence. For example:

> *X* Jack came to class late the teacher let him take the quiz anyway.

This sentence is punctuated like one sentence, but it is actually two sentences. To correct it, you need to separate the sentences with a period and capital letter.

> ➤ Jack came to class late. **T**he teacher let him take the quiz anyway.

A similar problem is a **comma splice**, which occurs when two or more sentences are separated by a comma instead of a period and a new sentence. For example:

> *X* The professor gave us another week to complete the term paper, we all applauded when she told us.

These two sentences need to be separated:

> ➤ The professor gave us another week to complete the term paper. **W**e all applauded when she told us.

Both run-on sentences and comma splices can also be corrected by adding a connector and the appropriate punctuation. For example:

> ➤ Jack came to class late, **but** the teacher let him take the quiz anyway.

> ➤ The professor gave us another week to complete the term paper. **Therefore,** we all applauded her.

> ➤ **Because** the professor gave us another week to complete the term paper, we all applauded her.

■ *PRACTICE 6:* **Correcting Run-on Sentences and Comma Splices**

Correct the punctuation in the following sentences. There may be more than one problem in each item. Compare your answers with a classmate.

1. Living in a dorm can be convenient and easy because you don't need a car you can walk to classes in a matter of minutes.

2. Weekends on campus are full of activities, such as sporting events and parties, students sometimes forget that weekends are also a time to catch up on class work.

3. Linguistics majors are required to take at least a year of a foreign language, it's important to study the grammar of another language besides English.

4. The dean was unhappy with all the construction on campus his office was being flooded with complaints from teachers and students alike.

(continued)

5. Many campuses have a study abroad department which can help students from the United States spend a year studying in another country, my roommate applied to go to China for a year, but she wasn't accepted she needed more credits.

6. Prak came from Cambodia to study pre-medicine and then medicine after he gets his degree, he'll return to his country to work with his father, who is a doctor in Phnom Penh.

7. Being on campus in the fall can be an exciting time, students have just returned from spending the summer at home, and everyone is excited about seeing each other again, students are even excited about starting classes again.

8. College football is a big business in the United States there are nearly two hundred teams playing in front of millions of people both in person and via television, in addition, millions of dollars are spent every weekend promoting the games and buying team souvenirs.

III LANGUAGE FOCUS

Commonly Confused Words: Verbs and Nouns

Both native and non-native speakers confuse the pairs of words below. Study the definitions and sample sentences to understand the difference between the two words in each pair.

1. **accept** *v.* to take something that is offered to you or to agree with something

   except *prep.* not included

   ➤ I can <u>accept</u> every argument that you make <u>except</u> the last one.

2. **adapt** *v.* to change to fit a new situation

   adopt *v.* to accept a suggestion

   ➤ In order to <u>adopt</u> my new class schedule, I had to <u>adapt</u> to getting up earlier.

3. **advice** *n.* an opinion you give to someone about what they should do

   advise *v.* to tell someone what you think they should do

   ➤ My professor <u>advised</u> me to take English Literature, and I took her <u>advice</u>.

4. **affect** *v.* to do something that causes a change in something or someone

   effect *n.* the way in which an event, act, or person changes someone or something

   ➤ The heavy snowstorm <u>affected</u> every business in town, including the university. The biggest <u>effect</u> was the university shutting down for a week.

5. **used to** *modal.* happening on a regular basis in the past

   be used to *v.* to be comfortable with a situation

   ➤ When I first became a teacher, I <u>used to</u> panic when I met a class for the first time, but now I <u>am used to</u> doing it, so it doesn't bother me as much.

6. **convince** *v.* to make someone feel certain that something is true

  persuade *v.* to make someone decide to do something

  ➤ My professor <u>convinced</u> me that global warming is happening, but she didn't <u>persuade</u> me to stop driving!

7. **imply** *v.* to suggest that something is true without saying or showing it directly

  infer *v.* to form an opinion that something is probably true based on information that you have

  ➤ The writer of the book <u>implied</u> that the theory was no longer valid, but I didn't <u>infer</u> that. My classmate pointed it out to me later.

■ PRACTICE 7: **Choosing the Correct Word**

Choose the correct word to go in each blank by circling it. Then compare your answers with a classmate.

Becoming an English Literature Major

My college counselor _____ me to take my first English
<u>(1. advice / advised)</u>

Literature class, which was the hardest class I ever took. First of all, it was at

eight o'clock every morning, and I _____ up so early. I finally
<u>(2. wasn't used to getting / didn't use to get)</u>

_____ to getting up early, but the habit did _____
<u>(3. adapted / adopted)</u>   <u>(4. affect / effect)</u>

my study time in the afternoon. I always needed a nap! Second, while

I enjoyed reading the books, I could never _____ what the
<u>(5. imply / infer)</u>

authors _____. This made me feel and look foolish in class.
<u>(6. were implying / were inferring)</u>

Everyone thought I was a poor student _____ my professor.
<u>(7. accept / except)</u>

For some reason, he believed that I would improve. At the end of the

semester, I was determined not to take another Lit class, but the professor

_____ me to take one more. The second English Literature class
<u>(8. convinced / persuaded)</u>

I ever took _____ me that I wanted to be an English Lit major.
<u>(9. convinced / persuaded)</u>

All in all, my college counselor and my first Literature professor had a big

_____ on my life.
<u>(10. affect / effect)</u>

Your Turn

Choose one of these typical problems that universities and students face. Then think of a solution to the problem. Finally, write an essay in which you discuss the benefits of, objections to, and counter-objections to your proposed solution. You may discuss these topics and possible solutions with a group of classmates to brainstorm ideas.

1. Foreign students have language difficulties in their classes.
2. Fewer and fewer students are enrolling in the university every year.
3. There is no money to have a music program.
4. There is not enough student housing.
5. It's difficult and expensive for students to park on campus.

Peer Help Worksheet

Trade essays and textbooks with a classmate. Read your classmate's essay while your classmate reads yours. Check off (✓) the items in your partner's book as you evaluate them. Then return the essays and books. If any of the items in your book are not checked off, and you agree with your partner, correct your essay before turning it in. Use a pencil if you write on your classmate's essay or book.

CONTENT

1 What is the problem that is presented? _____

_____

2 Is there a clear solution to the problem in the thesis
statement? . . . . ❏

3 Is the solution workable? . . . . ❏

4 How many benefits to the solution are discussed? _____

5 How many anticipated objections are there? _____

6 Have the objections been countered well? . . . . ❏

ORGANIZATION

1 Has the writer followed the appropriate organization pattern of a
problem and solution essay? . . . . ❏

2 What components does the concluding paragraph have? (Check all
that apply.)

    a. restatement of the proposal . . . . ❏

    b. summary of the benefits . . . . ❏

    c. final comment . . . . ❏

    d. call to action . . . . ❏

LANGUAGE

1 Has the writer avoided run-on sentences? . . . . ❏

2 Has the writer avoided sentences with comma splices? . . . . ❏

    If not, discuss any possible mistakes with the writer.

Writing to Communicate . . . More

As a journal entry or an in-class timed essay, choose one of the topics below. You
can choose to focus on writing fluently, or you can practice any of the organizational
techniques, sentence patterns, or language points discussed in this chapter.

1. Is there a problem at the school you are attending now or at a school you
   attended in the past that was solved? How was it solved? Was the solution
   effective? What other solutions might have worked?

2. College tuition is very expensive, and not all students can easily afford it. What
   are some solutions? Which solution do you think is the most practical?

3. What was missing from your university education in terms of preparing you
   for your chosen career? (Or, what was missing from your high school
   education in terms of preparing you for your university education?) Suggest
   how the university (or high school) might change its offerings to better
   prepare students for careers (or attending a university).

BRINGING IT ALL TOGETHER

I REVIEWING IDEAS

*Write **T** if the statement is true and **F** if the statement is false. Be prepared to explain your answers to a classmate.*

_____ 1. A predictor in a thesis statement indicates the number and/or the content of body paragraphs.

_____ 2. An introductory paragraph typically has three parts: a hook, a transition, and a thesis statement.

_____ 3. Every paragraph should have at least one irrelevant sentence.

_____ 4. For each objection you make in a problem and solution essay, there must be a counter-objection.

_____ 5. In a concluding paragraph, you must always include a restatement of the thesis statement, a summary of the body paragraphs, and a final comment.

_____ 6. A bridge connects the thesis statement to the first body paragraph.

_____ 7. One way to determine the cause of an event is to look at what happened directly before it.

_____ 8. The key to writing a good problem and solution essay is the popularity of the solution.

_____ 9. The topic sentence is to a paragraph what a thesis statement is to an essay.

_____ 10. You must always write about the causes before you write about the effects in a cause and effect essay.

II ERROR ANALYSIS

Identify the problem in each sentence with one of the abbreviations below. Then, working with a classmate, correct the sentences.

RO *run-on sentence*
CS *comma splice*
CH *choppy sentences*
ST *stringy sentences*

_____ 1. Before I moved to my new university, I thought about living in an apartment off campus, but I finally ended up living in a dorm, and I'm very glad I did because I'm meeting a lot of people and having a lot of fun, too.

_____ **2.** I studied Spanish in elementary school. I studied French in high school. I studied Spanish, French, and Dutch in a university. I studied Polish in graduate school. Now, I can only speak Spanish.

_____ **3.** My friend Jen used to play electric guitar in an all-girl band, now, unfortunately, she rarely picks up her guitar because she's so busy.

_____ **4.** Learning the pronunciation of a first language is much easier than learning the pronunciation in a second language if you are more than twelve years old it's almost impossible to master the native accent of a language.

_____ **5.** The guidance counselor came to our school last week to meet with everyone who wanted to go to a university, there were too many students for him to see in one day, so he's coming back next week.

_____ **6.** On our trip to Paris, we spent a lot of time in the Louvre Museum, and in London, we spent a lot of time in the Tower of London, but I think my favorite museum was the Hermitage in St. Petersburg in Russia, but I also liked the Vasa Museum in Stockholm.

_____ **7.** Many campuses have international dorms where only one foreign language is spoken students who live there have to speak the foreign language at all times.

_____ **8.** Post-Impressionism as a movement in painting began with Georges Seurat in the late 1800s. Paul Gauguin was a Post-Impressionist painter. Vincent Van Gogh was a Post-Impressionist painter. Paul Cezanne was a Post-Impressionist painter.

III LANGUAGE REVIEW

Choose the correct word to go in each blank by circling it. Then compare your answers with a classmate.

Stockholm's Vasa Museum

The Vasa Museum in Stockholm, Sweden, is quite _____ for
(1. interesting / interested)
its history and presentation. The Vasa was a seventeenth-century Viking ship

that sank on its first voyage. The _____ cause of its sinking
(2. immediate / likely)
was the overloading of passengers, goods, and cannons. The passengers

were saved _____ for a few unlucky people and the ship's cat.
(3. accept / except)
They _____ the overloaded ship. The Vasa remained underwater
(4. brought about / suffered the consequences of)
for over three hundred years. Then, in the 1920s and 1930s, a young boy's

interest in sunken treasure _____ his adult self to find the
(5. adopted / set the foundation for)

Vasa in 1956. Anders Franzén _____ the government to allow
(6. convinced / persuaded)
him to raise the Vasa. The Vasa was lifted from the sea in 1961, and it

became the centerpiece of a museum thirty years later. The _____
(7. appealing / appealed)
museum has a strong _____ on visitors because the items and
(8. affect / effect)
the ship itself are so well preserved. Walking on the ship gives you a real

feeling of how the Vikings _____. In short, if you go to
(9. used to live / were used to living)
Stockholm, my _____ is to not miss the Vasa Museum.
(10. advice / advise)

The Vasa Museum
Stockholm, Sweden

CHAPTER 4

SUMMARIZING AND RESPONDING

Gender Differences

I WRITING FOCUS

In Part I, you learned about the process of writing academic essays with information you already know. Another common academic writing assignment is **summarizing** an article from a newspaper, journal, or online Web site and including a personal **response** to what you have summarized.

Summarizing an Article

Summarizing is a skill in which you highlight the main ideas of an article. Its purpose is to demonstrate your understanding of what you have read. Here are some guidelines about summaries:

1. A summary only contains the main ideas from the article. You do NOT add your own ideas. You save your own ideas for the response.
2. A summary is always shorter than the original.
3. When you write a summary, you use your own words and grammar. You do NOT copy from the article, except for any technical words that are necessary.
4. Always include a reference to the source of the article within your summary.

Look at this example of a summary of one paragraph from a longer article about how men and women change as they get older.

Original	Summary
Original	**Summary**
As both genders age, however, their brains become more similar. "When you mature, you have to learn how to think both like a man and a woman," says [Dr. Malcolm] Stewart.	Men become more like women, and women become more like men as they get older, according to Lisa Martin ("Grasping the Gender Divide," *The Dallas Morning News*, August 21, 2007).
For men, that may mean a greater awareness of health issues. They also tend to be more nurturing as a grandfather than they were as a dad, plus they mellow both in terms of anger and their risk-taking behaviors. In the case of women, they "become more confident, more internally driven, more like their husbands," says Stewart.	
Excerpt from "Grasping the Gender Divide" by Lisa Martin *The Dallas Morning News* August 21, 2007	

main idea of paragraph →

source of article →

← summary of main idea of article

← source of article

■ PRACTICE 1: **Identifying Parts of a Summary**

Read the excerpt from an article on the left. Then select the better summary from the two on the right. Be prepared to explain your choice to a classmate. Circle the source citation in the summary.

1. This excerpt is from an article reporting on a speech given by Roy F. Baumeister at an American Psychological Association conference.

> The "single most underappreciated fact about gender," [Roy F. Baumeister] said, is the ratio of our male to female ancestors. While it's true that about half of all the people who ever lived were men, the typical male was much more likely than the typical woman to die without reproducing. Citing recent DNA research, Dr. Baumeister explained that today's human population is descended from twice as many women as men. Maybe 80 percent of women reproduced, whereas only 40 percent of men did.
>
> Excerpt from
> "Is There Anything Good About Men? and Other Tricky Questions"
> by John Tierney
> *The New York Times*
> August 20, 2007

A.

John Tierney wrote in an article in *The New York Times* ("Is There Anything Good About Men? and Other Tricky Questions," August 20, 2007) that people have more female ancestors than male ancestors because females were more likely to reproduce than males.

B.

John Tierney wrote in an article in *The New York Times* ("Is There Anything Good About Men? and Other Tricky Questions," August 20, 2007) that about 50% of the population is male and about 50% is female.

2. This excerpt is from an article about single-gender schooling, which is separating boys and girls into different classes.

> Research on the benefits of single-gender schooling isn't conclusive, but many practitioners say it works. Scott Phillipps, an academic dean at The Walker School in Marietta—where girls and boys have been taking middle school math classes separately for 15 years—has been studying the differences between high schoolers who took the single-gender classes and those who did not. He said he's found small but significant advantages in test scores for girls who took math without boys.
>
> Excerpt from
> "Single-Gender Classes a Growing Trend"
> by Bridget Gutierrez
> *The Atlanta Journal-Constitution,*
> September 1, 2007

A.

Even though there is not a scientific consensus about the benefits, separating girls and boys in middle school classes does seem to work in at least one school, reports Bridget Gutierrez in "Single-Gender Classes a Growing Trend" (*The Atlanta Journal-Constitution,* September 1, 2007).

B.

The Walker School in Marietta has had single-gender math classes for 15 years, reports Bridget Gutierrez in "Single-Gender Classes a Growing Trend" (*The Atlanta Journal-Constitution,* September 1, 2007).

What about you?

Do you think it's a good idea for children to be in single-gender classes? Share your opinion with a classmate.

The Process of Writing a Summary

There are several steps to writing a summary.

1. Read and Understand
   a. Before you read, quickly look over the title of the article, subheadings, and any pictures, diagrams, and notes that are not in the main article. This will start you thinking about what you will read.
   b. The first time you read the article, do not stop to look up words in the dictionary. When you finish, write down what you think the main idea of the article is. You may discover later that this is not the main idea, but this is where you start.
   c. On the second reading, look up any unfamiliar words that are necessary to understand the article. After you read the article the second time, check the main idea that you wrote earlier. Does it still seem like the main idea?
   d. Now read for the third time, again without a dictionary. Read as carefully as you can so that you have a good understanding of what the article is about.

2. Write the First Draft of the Summary

After reading, follow this procedure to write the summary:

a. Put the article aside.

b. Write down all the ideas that you remember from the article. It is important NOT to look at the article. It is too easy to copy from the article, and the summary must be in your own words.

c. Working from your notes, and NOT the article, write the summary using basic paragraph organization. In your topic sentence, include the author of the article (if any), the article title, the name of the newspaper or magazine, and the date of publication. The topic sentence could contain all this information, or you could use just one piece of this information and put the others in parentheses. Names of articles are put in quotation marks, and names of newspapers or magazines are italicized (or underlined if you are writing by hand). For example:

➤ In *The Dallas Morning News* article "Grasping the Gender Divide"
              publisher   title of article

(August 21, 2007), Lisa Martin said that men become more like women
   date   author

and women become more like men as they get older.

➤ In "Grasping the Gender Divide" (*The Dallas Morning News,*
      title of article   publisher

August 21, 2007), Lisa Martin said that men become more like women
  date   author

and women become more like men as they get older.

➤ Men become more like women and women become more like men as they get older, according to an article in *The Dallas Morning News* ("Grasping the
                                        publisher   title of article

Gender Divide" by Lisa Martin, August 21, 2007).
           author   date

The rest of the topic sentence contains the main idea of the article. The supporting sentences explain other important ideas from the article. You usually do not write a concluding sentence for a summary.

3. Check, Review, and Rewrite

When you have finished writing your summary, follow this procedure:

a. Reread the original article to double check that you have all the main ideas in your summary.

b. Be sure that your summary does not contain unnecessary details.

c. Check for grammar and punctuation mistakes.

d. Rewrite your summary if necessary.

■ **PRACTICE 2: Writing a Summary**

Follow the summary-writing procedure outlined on page 61. This summary will be of an entire article rather than a one-paragraph excerpt, but the guidelines are the same. As you go through each step, cover the box on the left and fill in the information in the box on the right. Then uncover the box on the left and check your answers.

➤ First reading (no dictionary)

She Says, He Says

by Erin Allday

Men, it turns out, talk just as much as women.

Sure, maybe guys talk more about cars and sports and the new iPhone, and women talk more about their feelings, but at the end of the day, each sex uses an average 16,000 words a day, say researchers who studied the conversational habits of 396 men and women for six years.

"I was a little surprised there wasn't any gender influence, because this stereotype of women talking more is such a powerful, popular idea," said Richard Slatcher, a doctoral candidate in psychology at the University of Texas and one of the

---

(continued)

16,215: Average number of words spoken by women per day
15,669: Average number of words spoken by men per day
564: Average number of words a day women spoke more than men in study

authors of the study. "But we were able to directly test the notion, and it's totally unfounded."

The study, results of which were published today in the journal *Science*, debunks an age-old assumption that women aren't just the fairer sex, they're the chattier one, too. The stereotype is so pervasive that even scientists have long assumed that women talk more, and they incorporated that assumption in psychological gender profiles.

Because conversations about relationships are often emotionally charged and intense, they take on more importance, as far as presumed word counts go, than they deserve, Mehl said.

"Because they feel so important, people overgeneralize from these conversations" and assume women are the ones doing the talking, Mehl said.

Mehl's study is not the first to analyze how much men and women talk, and previous studies have also suggested that there isn't much difference between the sexes. But earlier studies almost always recorded people in unnatural settings—sitting in a lab having a conversation, for example, when everyone knew scientists were listening.

The new study used audio clips from university students who agreed to be recorded for several days sometime between 1998 and 2004. The recording equipment amounted to mini-recorders and lapel microphones designed for studies that require listening to natural language use. The devices would turn on automatically for 30 seconds every 12.5 minutes, and the subjects could not control—and did not know—when the equipment was turned on or off.

There are some potential drawbacks to the study, namely that because it used only university students, it might not apply perfectly to men and women of all age groups and education levels. But Mehl said if there were important biological differences between men and women's verbosity, they would have registered at least somewhat in the study. As it was, women spoke on average about 546 more words each day than men, but that number was found to be not statistically significant.

Based on the study results, some stereotypes about conversational habits seemed to hold true, Mehl said. Researchers didn't actually count the types of words people used, but he said men tended to talk more about sports and technology and women about their feelings.

Previous studies have noted that women use more emotionally expressive language and describe things in relational terms—they use more pronouns, for example, said Slatcher. Men talk about more concrete things, he said.

San Francisco Chronicle, July 6, 2007. Reprinted with permission.

➤ Notes from the first reading:

Main idea:

Men and women talk the same amount—same number of words every day
Different than what people thought

Write the main idea here.

➤ Second reading:

Words to look up:

- notion = idea
- debunk = discredit
- chattier = more talkative
- pervasive = everywhere
- profiles = lists of characteristics
- verbosity = talking too much

Write down words you need to look up.

➤ Third reading:

Notes from article (not looking at the article):

- Men and women talk the same amount—almost same number of words every day
- Different than what people thought—stereotype is women talk much more than men
- People in study—college students
  - PROBLEM: students may not be representative, but scientists who did study say it is
- Men talk more about concrete stuff—women more about emotions

Write down other main ideas from the article that you remember. Do not look at the article when you do this.

➤ First draft:

A recent study found that men and women talk about the same amount. The results of the study were a surprise because, in general, people believe that women talk much more than men. The people who were studied were college students. Some people said that the group was not representative of the whole population, but the scientists in the study said it was. In general, men talk more about concrete things and women talk more about emotions.

Working from the notes you made above, write the first draft of your summary.

➤ Check the article:

Add reference to article

A recent study found that men

and women talk about the same

Identify study. What scientists? Add actual numbers?

amount. The results of the study

were a surprise because, in general,

people believe that women talk much

stereotypes—very old

more than men. The people who

were studied were college students.

Explain why better than former studies (not in lab)

Some people said that the group

was not representative of the whole

population, but the scientists in the

Necessary? Too much detail? Necessary?

study said it was. In general, men talk

more about concrete things and

women talk more about emotions.

Check your summary against the original article. Make notes here about the changes you want to make.

➤ Final draft:

The article "She Says, He Says" by Erin Allday (*San Francisco Chronicle, July 6, 2007*) reports on a study which found that men and women talk about the same amount. In fact, men and women both speak about 16,000 words each day. The results of the study were a surprise because, in general, people believe the old stereotype that women talk much more than men. The people who were studied were college students who had their conversations recorded at random. This was an improvement over earlier studies that only observed people in laboratory settings.

What about you?

Do you think it's true that men and women talk about the same amount? Why or why not? Share your answers with a classmate.

Write your final draft.

Responding to an Article

The companion paragraph to a summary is a response to the article. Remember that you do not add your ideas to the summary itself. Instead, put your reactions in the response paragraph. You can react by:

- agreeing or disagreeing with the conclusions that were made
- partially agreeing and partially disagreeing with the conclusions that were made
- reflecting on how your experiences relate to the points in the article
- analyzing the arguments
- objecting to methods used in the reporting

■ PRACTICE 3: **Identifying Parts of a Response**

Read these responses to the summary above. What types of reactions do the responses contain? Discuss your answers with a classmate.

1. My first reaction to this article is to disbelieve it. It is my experience that women do talk more than men. As a woman, I have always found it easier to talk to women because they tend to add a lot more details to what they are saying. The men I talk to usually talk in one- or two-word sentences. It isn't often that the men give me more information than I am interested in. However, the design of the study seems good to me because the men and women didn't know when they were being recorded. Therefore, this article has caused me to rethink my ideas about how much men and women talk in a day.

2.   I agree totally with this article. The stereotype that women talk more than men is just that—a stereotype. This article proves that by studying how people talk. The results of the study can be believed because the subjects were recorded in actual conversations and not in a laboratory. The only problem I see with this study is that it only recorded college students. Although the article said that they are representative of men and women in general, I'd like to see that proven. Therefore, maybe the next study should be expanded to include other groups of people.

II SENTENCE FOCUS

Reduced Adverbial Clauses

Adverbial clauses can be reduced to phrases to make your writing more sophisticated. Only adverbial clauses of time can be reduced, and only when the subjects of the adverbial clause and the independent clause are the same. There are two ways to reduce these adverbial clauses to phrases, depending on the verb phrase in the adverbial clause.

1. If the verb phrase has the auxiliary verb *be*, eliminate it and the subject of the adverbial clause.

   ➤ While ~~I was~~ studying psychology, I became fascinated by gender differences.

      ➤ While *studying* psychology, I became fascinated by gender differences.

   ➤ Once ~~it was~~ published, the book sold a million copies overnight.

      ➤ Once *published*, the book sold a million copies overnight.

2. If the verb phrase in the adverbial clause does not have the auxiliary *be*, change the verb into an *–ing* form and eliminate the subject of the adverbial clause.

   ➤ Before ~~we learned~~ Spanish, we studied French.

      ➤ Before *learning* Spanish, we studied French.

   ➤ Since ~~the archeologist~~ appeared on television, she has had many job offers.

      ➤ Since *appearing* on television, the archeologist has had many job offers.

■ PRACTICE 4: Reducing Adverbial Clauses

In the sentences below, reduce the adverbial clause if the conditions allow it. If the adverbial clause cannot be reduced, write X in the blank before the sentence.

——— 1. Before we found out the sex of our child, my husband decided that it was a boy, and I thought it was a girl.

——— 2. Although there are many differences in gender, these differences are small compared to the amount of similarities.

——— 3. The couples volunteered for the study before they knew the details.

——— 4. Women are perceived as being more approachable because they smile more and have a more relaxed posture.

——— 5. Since the year began, two new studies about the differences between male language and female language have been published.

———— **6.** When the study was finished, the results were published.

———— **7.** While my son was growing up, he wore only blue and green clothes.

———— **8.** After my daughter debated for months, she finally chose bright pink for her room color.

Reduced Adjective Clauses

Like adverbial clauses, adjective clauses (restrictive and non-restrictive) can also be reduced. This is another useful technique to make your writing more sophisticated. The ways to reduce an adjective clause are similar to the ways to reduce an adverbial clause.

1. Eliminate the subject relative pronoun of the adjective clause and the verb auxiliary verb *be*.

    ➤ The speaker ~~who was~~ delivering the lecture sounded familiar to me.

    > ➤ The speaker *delivering the lecture* sounded familiar to me.

    ➤ The psychology classes ~~that are~~ best attended are about the differences between men and women.

    > ➤ The psychology classes *best attended* are about the differences between men and women.

2. Eliminate the subject relative pronoun of the adjective clause and change the verb to the *–ing* form.

    ➤ Women ~~who~~ prefer the color blue to pink are in the minority.

    > ➤ Women *preferring* the color blue to pink are in the minority.

    ➤ My boss, ~~who arrived~~ late, apologized for the delay in starting the meeting.

    > ➤ My boss, *arriving* late, apologized for the delay in starting the meeting.

3. Adjective clauses can only be reduced when the relative pronoun in the adjective clause is a subject.

    ➤ Women ~~who~~ prefer the color blue to pink are in the minority.

    > ➤ Women *preferring* the color blue to pink are in the minority.

    ➤ Women whose favorite color is blue are in the minority.

    > ➤ No reduction possible.

    ➤ Women whom the study tested preferred pink.

    > ➤ No reduction possible.

■ PRACTICE 5: Reducing Adjective Clauses

In the sentences below, underline the adjective clause(s). Reduce the clauses if the conditions allow it.

1. Classes in gender differences, which are most commonly offered by psychology departments, are always quite crowded.

2. Research assistants actually counted the number of words that were spoken by men and women in the study.

(continued)

3. The result of the research clearly showed that women, whom people have long believed speak more than men, actually speak about the same amount as men.

4. I hope to get accepted by the university whose linguistic department has the foremost scholar on male/female language.

5. Some middle schools that separate boys and girls in classes are discovering the benefits of single-sex education.

6. Girls, who traditionally lag behind boys in math classes, demonstrate a better ability in math when boys aren't present in class.

7. The time when everyone believed that men talk less than women is past.

III LANGUAGE FOCUS

Reporting Words

When you include the reference to an article that you are summarizing, you need to use **reporting words** to cite the source of your summary within a sentence instead of in parentheses. Reporting words can be verbs or phrases.

Reporting Verbs

Many reporting verbs are neutral in meaning; that is, the writer simply indicates what the author is saying. These verbs are commonly used to introduce a summary or a paraphrase.

conclude	indicate	point out	say
explain	observe	report	state

These verbs can be used as the main verb in a sentence or in an adverb clause using the subordinating conjunction *as*.

➤ Allday *explains* that . . .   ➤ As Allday *points out*, . . .

➤ Allday *reports* that . . .   ➤ As Allday *indicates*, . . .

Other reporting verbs more clearly show the writer's opinion. For example:

argue	assert	claim	maintain

➤ Allday *argues* that . . .   Allday is arguing against a point of view, and her arguments are not commonly agreed on.

➤ Allday *asserts* that . . .   Allday is sure about what she is saying, but her ideas may not be commonly held.

➤ Allday *claims* that . . .   Allday is saying that something is a fact, and this belief is not commonly held, especially by the writer.

➤ Allday *maintains* that . . .   Allday has not changed her mind even though others disagree with her.

Reporting Phrases

Another way of referring to an article in your paper is to use one of these prepositional phrases followed by the name of the author, the title of the article, or the name of the publication.

> ➤ **According to** Allday, . . .

> ➤ **According to** "She Says, He Says," . . .

> ➤ **According to** the *San Francisco Chronicle,* . . .

> ➤ **In** Allday's article, she claims that . . .

> ➤ **In** "She Says, He Says," a study is described that . . .

> ➤ **In** the *San Francisco Chronicle,* Allday points out that . . .

■ PRACTICE 6: **Using Reporting Words**

Add reporting words to the supporting sentences below. Use the author's name, the title of the article (in quotation marks), the name of the publication (underlined), or any combination. Compare your answers with a classmate.

1. Even though people have had trouble believing it, it is true that people have more female ancestors than they do male ancestors.
   a. Author: John Tierney
   b. Title of article: The Missing Men in Your Family Tree
   c. Name of publication: The New York Times

2. In one Florida school, fifth-grade boys and girls are separated into two classes, where they are learning better.
   a. Author: Colleen Wixen
   b. Title of article: Same-Sex Classrooms Give Treasure Coast Students Opportunity to 'Be Themselves'
   c. Name of publication: TCPalm

3. Coffee seems to help elderly women avoid mental decline more than it helps elderly men.
   a. Author: Bernadine Healy, M.D.
   b. Title of article: Sex and the Mind's Decline
   c. Name of publication: U.S. News and World Report

4. Women read more books each year than men do, especially fiction books.
   a. Author: Eric Weiner
   b. Title of article: Why Women Read More than Men
   c. Name of publication: NPR.org

5. There are many differences in the nonverbal communication of men and women in terms of body movement, eye contact, touching, and personal space.
   a. Author: Judy Siennicki
   b. Title of article: Gender Differences in Nonverbal Communication
   c. Name of publication: colostate.edu

Your Turn

Your writing assignment is to write a one-paragraph summary of the following article from Washingtonpost.com, which was posted on August 20, 2007. Then write a one-paragraph response.

Girls Really Do Prefer Pink
by Ed Edelson

MONDAY, Aug. 20 (HealthDay News)—As the mother of a newborn baby girl, Dr. Anya C. Hurlbert wondered why all the products aimed at her daughter tended to have a pinkish tint.

As a professor of visual neuroscience at Newcastle University in England, Hurlbert was able to create a scientifically sound study to determine whether girls really do prefer pink. The answer, as outlined in a report in the Aug. 21 issue of the journal *Current Biology*, is "yes." Females do have a preference for pinkish colors that males don't.

"We find very clear differences between the males and females we have tested," Hurlbert said. "We haven't yet found any exceptions."

In more formal terms, females in the study showed a preference for the reddish side of the red-green axis of colors, while males didn't. There was no gender difference in preferences on the blue-yellow axis, with everyone tipping toward blue. The study included 208 participants, ranging in age from 20 to 26.

That bluish preference seems natural, Hurlbert said—blue skies and all that. The female tilt toward pink, she speculated, arose from evolutionary influences millions of years ago. "Females were the ones who gathered red fruit against a green background," she said. "Red is healthy in faces and in fruits."

The study Hurlbert did asked several hundred young men and women to make quick decisions on which color they preferred as pairs of colors flashed on a screen in front of them. "We did about a thousand different pairs," she noted.

While there has been speculation about a possible female preference for pink, "there has been very little hard evidence for sex differences," Hurlbert said. "We now have provided pretty robust and reliable evidence."

Peer Help Worksheet

Use this peer help worksheet to help your classmate check his or her summary. For further instructions, refer to page 19.

CONTENT

1 Does the summary include the main ideas of the article? ...... ❑

2 Does the summary include only information from the article and not any of the writer's ideas? .... ❑

3 Is the source of the summary included in the topic sentence? .. ❑

4 What does the response to the article include? (Check all that apply.)

    a. an agreement or disagreement with the article's conclusions . ❑

    b. a reflection on how the writer's experiences relate to the points in the article .... ❑

    c. an analysis of the arguments .... ❑

    d. an objection to methods used in the reporting .... ❑

ORGANIZATION

1 Is the summary organized as a paragraph? .... ❑

2 Is the response organized as a paragraph? .... ❑

LANGUAGE

1 Is the summary written with the writer's own words and grammar? .... ❑

2 Does the writer use appropriate reporting words? .... ❑

3 Has the writer used any reduced adverbial clauses correctly? .. ❑

4 Has the writer used any reduced adjective clauses correctly? .. ❑

Discuss any possible mistakes with the writer.

Writing to Communicate . . . More

For extra writing practice, choose a topic below. You can choose to focus on writing fluently, or you can practice any of the organizational techniques, language points, or sentence patterns discussed in this chapter.

1. Write your own reaction to the article "She Says, He Says" on pages 59–60.

2. As a journal entry or an in-class timed essay, choose one of the topics below.

    a. In what ways do gender differences play a part in your culture? In your life?

    b. Do you believe that men and women are equally capable? Why or why not?

3. As practice in writing summaries and responses, write a summary and response to an article from a recent newspaper or magazine. Be sure to submit the article to your teacher along with your summary and response.

The Kindness of Strangers

The Ring of
Brodgar,
Orkney Islands,
Scotland

I WRITING FOCUS

Writing a Narrative

A **narrative** is a story that can be used in academic writing as a hook in an introductory paragraph or as support in a body paragraph. As a hook, it is usually a short anecdote of an event that relates to the thesis statement. As support in a body paragraph, it is an extended, or **illustrative**, example. In both cases, the stories are used to support your thesis statement.

Use these techniques to include narratives in your writing:

1. Use **chronological order**. Describe events in the order in which they happened.

2. Use the **past tense** or the **present tense**. Using the present tense can make the story livelier, and readers can get the feeling that they are experiencing the story as it happens.

3. Use **dialogue** (with quotation marks) instead of reported speech to bring the story closer to readers.

Below is an excerpt from a short narrative by Fran Palumbo, who has traveled worldwide. This story is about an encounter she had with a local person in Scotland. As you read, think about Palumbo's use of chronological order, tense, and dialogue.

Excerpt 1

Highland Remedy
by Fran Palumbo

. . . Arriving at a modest building that looks like it might have been a small church in a previous incarnation, I walk in and head to the counter to order some food. In thick chalk letters, a blackboard menu overhead offers burgers, sandwiches, and soup. The room is Spartan[1] and honest like a Quaker[2] meeting room; the odor and hiss of fried food hangs in the air. I order the fish and chips, make a mental note to eat healthy tomorrow, and take a seat where the cheerful husband-and-wife owners direct me among the few tables scattered on the hardwood floor. The only other customer—an elfish, white-haired man in dark, baggy trousers and a windbreaker —who looks to be in his seventies, smiles shyly at me from the next table.

"Aye."[3] He nods in my direction. I nod back.

"You're not from around here, are ye?"[4]

"No," I confess. "From California. Just here traveling." Damn. I was hoping to blend in with the locals so no one would bother me. But at least I can understand him. Most of the Scots I've talked to, although only briefly, sound as if their tongues are always getting in the way of what they are trying to say.

"So, are ye plannin' to take the ferry to the Orkneys?"

"Well, no. I hadn't really thought about it. I'm just driving. Didn't think there was much to see there."

"Well, y'ought to consider it. Last year I was there and took the ferry on o'er and spent the day. It was lovely."

He launches into a guidebook-like monologue about the birdwatching and ancient sites—something called the Ring of Brodgar. I'm given directions and details on the ferry schedule and how to get to the attractions. . . .

A huge platter of fish and chips is placed in front of me and I can't shove the brown chunks into my mouth fast enough. After a few minutes, as if not to interrupt

(continued)

my eating, the old man rises from his table and, with a slight bow and twinkle in his eye, shakes my hand and tells me he enjoyed talking to me.

It's getting late and I want to get back to the motel, take a walk down to the water and catch the sunset, so I devour the rest of my meal and head up to the counter to pay. The owner waves away the bills I hold out.

"It's paid for," he tells me. I am confused.

"The ol' man paid for you when he left."

Amazed that a stranger would pay for my dinner then leave without any acknowledgement of his kindness, I smile and think, "How sweet." No one has ever done this before on any of my travels, and I am incredibly touched. All of these months, after feeling that every single person I encountered was a living, breathing "give-me" machine, I meet one person in a remote corner of the world who gives just for the sake of giving, wanting nothing in return, not even a "thank you." This small gesture is, ironically, larger than he will ever know. . . .

———

Reproduced with permission from *The Kindness of Strangers* (edited by Don George), Lonely Planet, © 2003 Lonely Planet Publications.

[1]**Spartan** *adj.* the condition of existing simply and without comfort

[2]**Quaker** *adj.* belonging to a Christian religious group

[3]**aye** *adv.* yes

[4]**ye** *pron.* you (in old use)

■ PRACTICE 1: **Analyzing Excerpt 1**

With a classmate, discuss these questions. Find specific lines in the excerpt that support your answers.

1. How are the events of the story told? How are the sentences ordered?

2. What tense is used to tell the story? Why did the author decide to use this tense?

3. How does the author use dialogue? How does the use of dialogue add to the story?

4. What was the author's purpose in writing this story?

5. How might someone use this is an academic paper?

What about you?

Have strangers been kind to you when you have traveled to another city or country? How so or how not? Share your answer with a classmate.

Responding to a Travel Story

In Chapter 4, you learned several ways of responding to the content in an article you summarized. Three of these ways are applicable for responding to a travel story:

● agreeing or disagreeing with the conclusions (if any) that were made

● partially agreeing and partially disagreeing with the conclusions (if any) that were made

● reflecting on how your experiences relate to the points in the article

Notice the use of the present tense to refer to someone else's writing:

➤ Palumbo *describes* meeting a Scot on her travels.

As you read the response to the travel story, identify the types of responses that the writer uses.

In "Highland Remedy," Fran Palumbo comes to the conclusion that there are still people in the world that will give without expecting anything in return. After she describes an encounter with an old Scotsman, she writes, "All of these months, after feeling that every single person I encountered was a living, breathing 'give-me' machine, I meet one person in a remote corner of the world who gives just for the sake of giving, wanting nothing in return, not even a 'thank you'" (George, 2003, p. 56). This amazes her. I can relate to this amazement because I also had a similar travel experience in which a stranger did something for me and expected nothing in return. Several years ago, I was traveling across the United States by train. I didn't have much money, so I didn't spend a lot on food. On a two-day train ride, I was sitting across the aisle from a man who was probably my father's age. We occasionally shared an observation about the land that we were traveling through. For every meal, he would get up and go to the dining car to eat, and I would get out my crackers and cheese, or yogurt and fruit. He saw that I was mostly eating crackers by the end of the second day and brought me some milk and a sandwich. He laid it on the seat next to me and mumbled something about my needing protein. I thanked him, but he left the train so quickly, I wasn't sure that he'd heard me. His kindness has stayed with me all these years just as Palumbo's Scotsman has stayed with her.

Using Quotations from Outside Sources

In the response above, the writer uses a quotation from the short story to emphasize the main idea of the response. Using a quotation is a good way to incorporate information from outside sources into your writing.

Rules for Using Quotations

1. Use quotations when the author has a unique way of saying or describing something.
2. Use quotations when something would be lost by summarizing or paraphrasing the passage.

3. Copy direct quotations exactly.

4. Use quotation marks and a reporting word. (See Chapter 4, pages 66–67, for a list of reporting words). The reporting word can go at the beginning, middle, or end of the quotation.

Rules for Using Quotation Marks

1. For each sentence you quote, begin with a capital letter regardless of where the reporting phrase goes.

   ➤ Palumbo says in her travel story, "**T**his small gesture is, ironically, larger than he will ever know."

2. When the reporting phrase comes in the middle of the sentence, it is set off by commas, and the second part of the sentence does not begin with a capital letter.

   ➤ "The room is Spartan and honest," according to Palumbo, "**l**ike a Quaker meeting room; the odor and hiss of fried food hangs in the air."

3. Periods and commas are always inside the quotation marks.

   ➤ "A huge platter of fish and chips is placed in front of me**,**" Palumbo writes, "and I can't shove the brown chunks into my mouth fast enough**.**"

4. When your quotation is more than forty words, indent it. Do not use quotation marks. The reporting phrase is part of your paragraph and is followed by a colon.

   ➤ In her story, Palumbo describes the scene when the old Scot left:

   > A huge platter of fish and chips is placed in front of me and I can't shove the brown chunks into my mouth fast enough. After a few minutes, as if not to interrupt my eating, the old man rises from his table and, with a slight bow and twinkle in his eye, shakes my hand and tells me he enjoyed talking to me.

5. Use single quotation marks to indicate a quotation within a quotation.

   ➤ Palumbo continues, "Amazed that a stranger would pay for my dinner then leave without any acknowledgement of his kindness, I smile and think, 'How sweet.'"

■ PRACTICE 3: Using Quotation Marks

For each item below from Palumbo's story, insert a reporting phrase and quotation marks. Make any necessary changes.

1. I order the fish and chips, make a mental note to eat healthy tomorrow, and take a seat where the cheerful husband-and-wife owners direct me among the few tables scattered on the hardwood floor.

2. I was hoping to blend in with the locals so no one would bother me. But at least I can understand him. Most of the Scots I've talked to, although only briefly, sound as if their tongues are always getting in the way of what they are trying to say.

3. "Last year I was there and took the ferry on o'er and spent the day. It was lovely."

4. He launches into a guidebook-like monologue about the birdwatching and ancient sites—something called the Ring of Brodgar. *(Put the reporting phrase in the middle of the sentence)*.

Using Brackets and Ellipses

You may need to add a word or two to your quotation to make it fit in grammatically with your sentence or to explain a word or phrase. Put your own writing in **brackets** ([ ]) within the quoted material. Brackets indicate that you are adding something to the quotation.

Original sentence:	Arriving at a modest building that looks like it might have been a small church in a previous incarnation, I walk in and head to the counter to order some food.
Quoted:	Palumbo describes the building as simple and "look[ing] like it might have been a small church in a previous incarnation [time period] . . ."

Sometimes, you need only part of a sentence for your quotation. To indicate that you are leaving out a part of a quotation, use **ellipses** (. . .).

Original sentence:	The only other customer—an elfish, white-haired man in dark, baggy trousers and a windbreaker—who looks to be in his seventies, smiles shyly at me from the next table.
Quoted:	Palumbo writes, "The only other customer . . . smiles shyly at me from the next table."

■ PRACTICE 4: Using Brackets and Ellipses

Insert part of the given original sentence into each sentence below. Make the quotation fit into the sentence structure and be sure that it makes sense. Use quotation marks correctly.

1. *Original sentences:* "Aye." He nods in my direction. I nod back. "You're not from around here, are ye?"

   Palumbo shows us the quaint speech of the elderly Scot with phrases such as _____ and

   _____.

2. *Original sentence:* After a few minutes, as if not to interrupt my eating, the old man rises from his table and, with a slight bow and twinkle in his eye, shakes my hand and tells me he enjoyed talking to me.

   Palumbo describes the old Scot as having _____, which proved that despite his age, he was quite alert.

3. *Original sentence:* This small gesture is, ironically, larger than he will ever know . . .

   Palumbo is very touched by the fact that the Scot paid for her dinner without telling her. She describes this kindness as _____
   _____.

4. *Original sentence:* A huge platter of fish and chips is placed in front of me and I can't shove the brown chunks into my mouth fast enough.

   Palumbo was very hungry and says, _____
   _____.

Incorporating Outside Information into Your Writing

As you learned above, you can support your own ideas by incorporating quotations from outside sources into your writing. In fact, in many academic writing assignments, professors *expect* students to support their ideas and arguments with information from outside sources.

Avoiding Plagiarism

Before you learn more about the techniques of incorporating other people's writing into your own, it is important to understand the concept of **plagiarism**. Plagiarism happens when you take some information, ideas, or special language from another source and use it in your writing without saying where you got the information. Plagiarism is a serious offense in high schools, colleges, and universities in many countries. In fact, students can fail a class or be expelled from their school if they are caught plagiarizing. The good news is that plagiarism can easily be avoided by properly identifying your sources.

The way that you do that is to **document*** your sources and use quotations marks to signal direct quotations. Documenting means to include a references list at the end of your paper and cite each reference you use in the body of your paper. You will practice documenting quotations in this chapter and practice documenting paraphrases in Chapter 6.

Making a References List

A **References** list is a formal list of the sources that you used. It is on a separate page after the last page of your essay. Each item in a References list is called an **entry**, and the entries are placed in alphabetical order according to the first word in the entries. (Use the second word if the first word is *a, an,* or *the.*) Look at the following basic entry formats. Note that for titles of all sources you only use a capital letter for the first word and the first word after a colon. All other words (except proper nouns) are not capitalized.

---

*The style of documentation taught throughout this book is that of the American Psychological Association (APA).

Abbreviations Used in the Explanations Below

- ALN   author's last name
- AI   author's first name initial
- ELN   editor's last name
- EI   editor's first name initial
- n.d.   no date
- url   universal resource locator (the address of a Web site)

Definitions Used in the Explanations Below

- Volume   A grouping of individual magazines or journals
- Issue   An individual magazine or journal
- Posting date   The date that something is added to a Web site
- Retrieved   The date that something is accessed or read

Basic Entry Format for a Book

1. One author

ALN, AI. (Year). *Book title.*
Place of publication:
Publisher.

Cooper, A. (2006). *Dispatches from the edge.* New York: HarperCollins Publishers.

Use last name, first initial for the first author followed by a comma and an ampersand (&) and the second author's last name and first initial followed by a period. If there are three to six authors, use commas between the authors' names. Add an ampersand before the last name only. If there are more than six authors, use a comma after the last one and "et al." Everything else remains the same.

2. More than one author

ALN, AI., & ALN, AI. (Year).
Book title. Place of publication:
Publisher.

Keith, S., & Proenneke, R. (2003). *One man's wilderness: An Alaskan odyssey.* Portland, OR: Alaska Northwest Books.

3. Editor

ELN, EI. (Ed.). (Year). *Book title.*
Place of publication: Publisher.

McCauley, L. (Ed.). (2005). *The best women's travel writing.* Berkeley: Publishers Group West.

4. Chapter within a book by an editor

ALN, AFI. (date). Title of chapter.
In EFI ELN (Ed.), *Title of book* (page numbers).
Place of publication:
Publisher.

Waters, A. (2003). Tea and cheese in Turkey. In D. George (Ed.), *The kindness of strangers* (pp. 41–43). Melbourne: Lonely Planet Publications.

Basic Entry Format for a Journal Article

A volume is all the issues of a journal for a year. Some journals continue the page numbers from one issue to the next. Other journals start new page numbers for each issue.

1. Page numbers are continuous throughout the year.

ALN, AI., & ALN, AI. (Year). Title of article. *Name of publication, Volume number,* pages.

Pan, S., & Ryan, C. (2007). Gender, framing and travelogues. *Journal of Travel Research, 45,* 464.

2. Page numbers start from 1 in each issue.

ALN, AI. (Year). Name of article. *Name of publication, Volume number* (Issue number), pages.

Lukinbeal, C. (2005). Cinematic landscapes. *Journal of Cultural Geography, 23* (1), 3.

Basic Entry Format for a Magazine Article

1. One author

ALN, AI. (year, month day). Title of article. *Name of magazine, Volume number,* pages.

Heron, M. (2007, February). A terrible case of itchy feet. *Geographical, 79,* 90.

2. No author

Title of article (year, month day). *Name of magazine, Volume number,* pages.

The mother of all travelogues. (2005, December). *Photo District News, 25,* 104.

Basic Entry Format for a Newspaper Article

Use "p." to indicate one page and "pp." to indicate two or more pages.

1. One author

ALN, AI. (year, month day). Title of article. *Name of newspaper,* pages.

Olster, A. I. (2007, October 14). Unwelcome drama in fall tourism. *Boston Globe,* p. 4.

2. No author

Title of article (year, month day). *Name of newspaper,* pages.

Grounded expectations. (2008, January 7). *Bangor Daily News,* p. 6.

Basic Entry Format for a Web Site

Note: Divide urls before or after a slash.

---

1. General web page

ALN, AI. (posting date). Title of page. Retrieved month day, year from http://complete url.

Rocha, G. (2007, August 3). Bum tourism in Bratislava. Retrieved September 8, 2007 from http://www.roadjunky .com/article/1471/ bum-tourism-in-bratislava.

2. Online periodicals

ALN, AI. (date of publication). Title of article. *Title of online publication*. Retrieved month day, year from http://complete url.

Keillor, G. (2008, January 2). Just follow the map. *Salon.com*. Retrieved January 11, 2008 from http://www.salon.com/opinion/ keillor/2008/01/02/map/ index.html?source=rss&aim=/ opinion/keillor.

3. Online periodicals with no posting date

ALN, AI. (n.d.). Title of article. *Title of online publication*. Retrieved month day, year from http://complete url.

Power, M. (n.d.). Hiking the Great Wall: Astride the dragon's back. *NationalGeographic.com*. Retrieved September 8, 2007 from http://nationalgeographic .com/adventure/0510/features/ hiking_great_wall.html.

■ PRACTICE 5: Creating a References List

Below is information from four sources. Create a References list. Remember to alphabetize and indent your list appropriately.

Source 1 (Book)

- Author: Barry Lopez
- Title: Resistance
- Date of publication: 2004
- Place of publication: New York
- Publisher: Alfred A. Knopf

Source 2 (Magazine)

- Author: Keith Bellows
- Title: Sailing with a Pioneer
- Periodical: National Geographic Traveler
- Date: September 2007
- Volume: 24
- Page: 36

Source 3 (Web site)

- Author: Daisann McLane
- Title of article: A Very Long Way to the Hong Kong Café
- Date of posting: March 21, 2007
- Name of Web site: World Hum
- url: http://www.worldhum.com/dispatches/item/a_very_long_way_to_the_hong_kong_cafe_20070315/
- Date of access: September 9, 2007

Source 4 (Journal)

- Author: none
- Title of article: Historical Cemeteries Court Tourists
- Name of journal: American History
- Volume: 42
- Issue: 4
- Date: October 2007
- Page: 13

In-Text Citations

Each time you use a quotation, a paraphrase (see Chapter 6), or a summary (see Chapter 4) in the text of your paper, you must give credit to the source in the text of your paper with an **in-text citation**. These citations go after the sentence that includes the cited information. The basic citation is the author's last name (or shortened title if there is no author) and the date of publication. In addition, with a quotation, you need to indicate the page number. In this sentence taken from the response paragraph on page 73, you can see the citation after the quotation. Notice that the period goes after the citation.

> After she describes an encounter with an old Scotsman, she writes, "All of these months, after feeling that every single person I encountered was a living, breathing 'give-me' machine, I meet one person in a remote corner of the world who gives just for the sake of giving, wanting nothing in return, not even a 'thank you' " (George, 2003, p. 56).

Each citation must correspond to an entry in the References list at the end of the paper. Below is a sample References list and the corresponding in-text citation for each entry.

References

Charleston, R. (2007, October 7). Moscow offers history, art—and McDonald's. *Philadelphia Tribune*, pp. T26-T29.

De Gues, P. (n.d.) From the Slovenian Alps to Lake Balaton. *Off the Beaten Track*. Retrieved September 9, 2007 from http://www.off-the-beaten-track.net/.

In-Text Citations

(Charleston, 2007, p. T27)
Note: If you directly quote from a source, you need to indicate the page number.

(De Gues, n.d.)
Note: If there is no date, use n.d. as if it were a date.

The heart and soul of Morocco. (2007, July 13). *The Week, 7,* p. 34.

("The Heart," 2007)
Note: If there is no author, use an abbreviated title in quotation marks followed by a comma and the year. Do not use months or days.

Schultz, P. (2003). *1000 places to see before you die.* New York: Workman Publishing Company, Inc.

(Schultz, 2003)
Note: Use the author's last name followed by a comma and a date. If there are two authors, use both last names. If there are three to five authors, use the last names only on their first citation. After that, use the first author's last name plus *et al.*

■ PRACTICE 6: Writing In-Text Citations

Write an in-text citation for an imaginary quote for each entry in the References list below.

A wilderness on the lower Mississippi. (2007, September 7). *The Week, 7,* 34.

Krakauer, J., & Roberts, D. (1999). *Iceland: Land of the sagas.* New York: Villard Books.

Lopez, B. (1994). *Field notes.* New York: Vintage Books.

Pfeiff, M. (2008, January 6). Sailing the Andes: Ferry and bus rides cross South America's lofty spine. *San Francisco Chronicle,* p. G1.

Rosenthal, J. (2007, September). Chilling on the Pacific Coast. *National Geographic Traveler, 24* (7), 66.

Somerville, M. (2007, March 30). Budget travel tips you'll never read in a guidebook. *Brave New Traveler.* Retrieved September 9, 2008 from http://www.bravenewtraveler.com/author/madeline-somerville/.

II SENTENCE FOCUS

More on Reduced Adverbial and Adjective Clauses

In Chapter 4, you learned how to reduce **adverbial clauses** to vary your sentence structure. For example:

➤ I became fascinated by Cambodia *while I was reading a travelogue on the country.*

→ I became fascinated by Cambodia *while reading a travelogue on the country.*

Another variation is to eliminate *while* from the sentence with no change in meaning. The reduced adverbial clause is often moved to the front of the sentence.

> → *Reading the travelogue on Cambodia,* I became fascinated by the country.

This reduction can also occur when *because* is the subordinator of the adverbial clause.

> ➤ We had to come home early *because we ran out of money.*

> → *Running out of money,* we had to come home early.

Adjective clauses can also be reduced and moved to the beginning of the sentence. For example:

> ➤ The Taj Mahal, *which attracts nearly three million tourists annually,* is the most popular tourist attraction in India.

> ➤ The Taj Mahal, *attracting nearly three million tourists annually,* is the most popular tourist attraction in India.

> ➤ *Attracting nearly three million tourists annually,* the Taj Mahal is the most popular tourist attraction in India.

■ **PRACTICE 7: Moving Reduced Adverbial and Adjective Clauses**

Reduce the adverbial or adjective clause in each sentence below. Then move it to the beginning of the sentence.

1. Denver, which is called the Mile-High City, is worth visiting on a tour of the United States.

2. The woman looked very traditional because she was wearing a kimono.

3. While she was flying for the first time, Farisa felt nervous.

4. The Senegalese dancers, who performed after sunset, took advantage of the dark to make their performance magical.

5. While we were exploring the caves at Lascaux, we saw many ancient cave drawings.

6. Junichi, who came to the airport two hours early, was frustrated to discover that his plane was delayed for five hours.

Avoiding Dangling Modifiers

The reduced adverbial and adjective clauses above are also called **modifiers** because they modify, or describe, the subject in each independent clause. Make sure that the modifier has the same underlying subject as the independent clause. If it has a different subject, it is called a **dangling modifier** and can lead to misunderstandings. For example, notice how this sentence changes meaning if the modifier is left dangling:

> ➤ *While I was writing down the address,* the bus left me standing in the street.

> ✗ *Writing down the address,* the bus left me standing on the street.

This sounds as though the bus was writing, which of course is impossible! The correct use of the modifier requires that you change the independent clause.

> ➤ *Writing down the address,* I was left on the street by the bus.

■ *PRACTICE 8:* **Identifying and Correcting Dangling Modifiers**

Identify the modifier in each sentence below by underlining it. If it is correct, write C in the blank. If it is dangling, write DM in the blank, and correct the sentence so that the modifier is correct.

_____ **1.** Camping under the stars on the beach, the sound of the waves lulled us to sleep.

_____ **2.** Explaining the history of the caves, Lily and Alice learned a lot from the tour guide.

_____ **3.** Tired of listening to the noise through the open window, Kyungho reluctantly closed it.

_____ **4.** Having just bought a plane ticket, the news of the hurricane was broadcast.

_____ **5.** Finishing work late, the taxi was waiting for me when I got to the corner.

_____ **6.** Arriving thirteen hours late, the passengers were tired and upset.

III LANGUAGE FOCUS

Phrases for Agreeing and Disagreeing

When you write a response to a reading, you give your opinion, which includes those points you agree with and those points you disagree with. To make your writing more sophisticated, use a variety of phrases to indicate your agreement or disagreement. Below is a list of verbs and verb phrases and sample sentences:

TO AGREE	Sample Sentences
be in agreement with	➤ I am **in agreement with** you about airline travel. ➤ I am **in agreement with** your statement that airline travel is awful these days.
concur with	➤ I **concur with** the decision to go by train. ➤ I **concur with** the idea that train travel is pleasant.
have the same opinion	➤ I **have the same opinion** about ocean cruises as you do. ➤ We **have the same opinion** that ocean cruises are the best way to relax.

TO DISAGREE	Example Sentences
dispute	➤ I *dispute* the author's basic assumption. ➤ I *dispute* the author's basic assumption that all airlines disregard environmental concerns.
object to	➤ I *object to* the ideas in the article. ➤ I *object to* the idea that traveling is just for the rich.
take issue with	➤ I *take issue with* your argument. ➤ I *take issue with* your argument that train travel is boring.

■ *PRACTICE 9*: **Using Verb Phrases of Agreement and Disagreement**

Write sentences in which you agree or disagree with the following statements. Use one of the verb phrases above in each sentence.

1. A vacation in the tropics is the only way to rest and relax.

2. Work weeks should be four days.

3. Eco-cruises offer an up-close and personal view of the world.

4. People in most countries are friendly and helpful to tourists.

5. It's impossible to have fun on a camping trip.

6. Armchair traveling can be as thrilling as real traveling.

7. A skiing trip in the Alps is an exhausting vacation.

8. It's best to travel with a group.

Phrases for Hedging

You might not totally agree or totally disagree with what someone has said or written. In this case, you can use **hedging phrases**. These are phrases which can qualify your statement and also make it seem less rude or offensive.

To Introduce Noun Clauses	Adverbs	To Begin a Sentence
It's possible that. . . It's not impossible that. . . I believe that. . .	almost always more or less (not) necessarily probably somewhat usually	As some see it, In general, Strictly speaking,

> ➤ Going by boat isn't *necessarily* the best way to go.

> ➤ *It's possible that* what you are saying isn't true.

> ➤ We could *probably* visit Bangkok if we had time.

> ➤ *In general*, travel is more challenging with young children.

■ PRACTICE 10: Using Hedging Phrases

Insert a hedging phrase in the sentences below to make them sound less harsh. Compare your answers with a classmate.

1. Traveling cheaply means traveling uncomfortably.

2. Armchair travelers don't get an appreciation for a location.

3. Five-star hotels are too expensive.

4. Traveling alone is sad.

5. A cruise on a 5000-passenger ship is not peaceful or relaxing.

6. To stay safe on the streets of a large foreign city, you shouldn't go out without a travel guide.

7. August is the worst month to visit the Grand Canyon because of the heat.

8. Cairo is a confusing city for tourists.

IV WRITING TO COMMUNICATE

Your Turn

For your writing assignment, write a summary and response paragraph to the travelogue on page 86.

1. Summarize in two or three sentences what happened to Jan Morris in St. Petersburg. Respond to what Jan Morris says about the kindness of strangers by writing your own story as an example to support your response.

2. Which sentence is the main idea of what Morris is saying about the kindness of strangers? Incorporate this sentence into your paragraph by quoting it and citing the source.

3. Include a References page. Use this information:
   Title of book: *The Kindness of Strangers*
   Editor: Don George
   Date of publication: 2003
   Place of publication: Melbourne
   Publisher: Lonely Planet Publications

The Matter of Kindness
by Jan Morris

A year or two ago, on a wet morning, I fell over in the filthily potholed Haymarket in St. Petersburg, Russia. . . . *What* a mess I was in! My jeans were torn, I was dripping with mud, my books, bag and papers were strewn[1] all over the place, and for the life of me I couldn't get up again. . . .

A citizen . . . was there to save me. He helped me to my feet. He gathered my scattered possessions. He took me to his shabby neighboring apartment, and while he brushed down my coat and scrubbed my shoes, allowed me to wash myself in his far from luxurious bathroom. Having found some antiseptic for my grazed[2] knee, he made me coffee and saw me solicitously[3] down to the street. I have never seen him again, but I have come to think of him since as half-mythical.

I suppose that most travelers have experienced the kindness of strangers at one time or another, and I am not alone, I am sure, in thinking of it in allegorical[4] terms. Good Samaritans are familiar figures of art and fable. They enter narratives sidelong, out of the mist, or they are glimpsed across empty landscapes, or they arrive melodramatically at the moment of climax, or they snatch unfortunates out of city mud.

And then they disappear. For the point about them is that they *are* strangers. They come, do something helpful, and go away. They are the emblematic[5] emissaries of Kindness, with a capital K.

---

[1]**strewn** *past participle of "strew,"* to scatter things around a large area

[2]**graze** *v.* to break the surface of your skin by rubbing it across something rough

[3]**solicitously** *adv.* caring very much about someone's safety, health, or comfort while helping them

[4]**allegorical** *adj.* having a concrete representation of an abstract idea

[5]**emblematic** *adj.* seeming to represent or be a sign of something

Peer Help Worksheet

Use this peer help worksheet to help your classmate proofread his or her summary. For further instructions, refer to page 19.

CONTENT

1 Does the summary include the main ideas of the article? ...... ❑

2 Does the response to the article include a personal story from the writer's experience? .... ❑

3 Does the paragraph quote a relevant sentence from the article? . ❑

4 Is the quotation cited correctly? .... ❑

ORGANIZATION

1 Is the paragraph organized well (with a topic sentence, etc.)? .. ❑

2 Is the quotation incorporated appropriately? .... ❑

LANGUAGE

1 Is the summary written with the writer's own words and grammar? .... ❑

2 Does the writer use appropriate reporting words? .... ❑

3 Does the writer use reduced clauses correctly? .... ❑

4 Does the write use hedging phrases where necessary? .... ❑

Discuss any possible mistakes with the writer.

Writing to Communicate . . . More

As a journal entry or an in-class essay, choose a topic below. You can choose to focus on writing fluently, or you can practice any of the organizational techniques, sentence patterns, or language points discussed in this chapter.

1. Another adventure that you had while traveling and what you learned from it
2. A lesson that you learned from a stranger
3. A trip that you want to take and your reasons for wanting to take it
4. A movie or book that you like about traveling and some points it makes or lessons it teaches

TWO SIDES OF AN ISSUE: RESPONDING WITH PARAPHRASING

Generation Y: Hardworking or Spoiled?

I WRITING FOCUS

Identifying Arguments

In an academic setting, you will often be required to argue for or against one side of a **controversial issue**. A controversial issue is one in which there are two distinct views—one **pro** (in favor of) and one **con** (against). Examples of issues with two sides are the use of nuclear energy, the use of animals in medical testing, and genetic engineering.

You may be asked to write an essay in which you respond to one or two articles on a particular controversial issue. In this case, you need to support one side of the controversy and discuss the reasons for your beliefs.

■ PRACTICE 1: Identifying Controversial Issues

*Write **C** if the thesis statement is controversial. Write **NC** if the thesis statement is not controversial. Discuss your answers with a classmate.*

_____ 1. There are many kinds of animal habitats.

_____ 2. Terminally ill people should be allowed to ask their doctors to help them die.

_____ 3. Despite the Constitution prohibiting censorship, it should be forbidden to criticize the president in a time of war.

_____ 4. The new class schedule offers many new and fascinating classes.

_____ 5. People are homeless because they don't want to work.

_____ 6. The media is doing a poor job of keeping citizens informed.

Background Information

Below you will read two articles about high school valedictorians. The valedictorian in a high school is traditionally the best student academically. This student delivers the valedictory, a farewell speech at the graduation ceremony.

In order to choose a valedictorian, the high school adminstration considers:

1. Grade point average (or GPA). The grade point average is a numerical equivalent of letter grades. A letter grade of A is worth four points, a grade of B is worth three points, a C is worth two points, and a D is worth 1 point. For example, if a student takes five classes and receives two As, two Bs, and a C, his or her grade point average will be 3.2.

2. The number of Advanced Placement (or AP) classes. These academically advanced classes are designed for students planning to attend a university. At some schools, grades from these classes carry a higher point value than grades in regular classes.

■ PRACTICE 2: Comparing Honors

Discuss the answers to these questions with a classmate or small group.

1. Are (Were) academically superior students honored at graduation in your high school? If so, how? What are (were) the criteria for choosing this student?

2. What are some advantages and disadvantages to honoring the top academic student?

3. Should other types of students be honored in high school? If so, what types of students? Why and how should they be honored?

Article 1

Schools Playing Down Valedictorian Honors
by Marissa DeCuir

Keely Breen aspired[1] to be her high school valedictorian. But, Vermont's Burlington High School made the decision to no longer name valedictorians at the end of Breen's junior year, stripping[2] the 18-year-old of the title she would have had on June 15. "At first, it did bug[3] me. I wasn't really happy about it," Breen says. "To enter

5 high school with that as a goal and have it taken away from you, that's hard."

Valedictorians have become less prominent at graduation ceremonies across the USA. Nat Harrington, spokesman for the Palm Beach County (Fla.) School District, says that's a positive development because the fight for the title has gotten out of hand.

"The student's mom comes in
10 the first day of school to find out what her daughter needs to do to become valedictorian," he says.

Educators and students
15 say pursuit of the top grade point average (GPA) has distorted[4] the academic process: Students might transfer to schools perceived

20 as easier, or they may drop enriching courses in music or arts to grab advanced courses that have a higher weighted GPA.

"The competition is ridiculous," says Sage Snider, 17, a senior at Severna Park High School in Maryland. "It doesn't make sense. It's completely unfair for so many." Snider ranks[5] fourth in her class. "I went down this year because I took
25 orchestra," she says. A fellow student dropped it to pick up a weighted Advanced Placement (AP) course.

Minnesota's Eden Prairie High School selected 24 valedictorians this month based on students with a 4.0 GPA. Next year's top graduates will be those who
29 complete at least six AP courses and achieve a 3.5 cumulative GPA.

USA TODAY. June 28, 2007. Reprinted with permission.

---

[1]aspire *v.* to have a strong desire to achieve something

[2]strip (someone) of (something) *v.* to take away something important from someone

[3]bug *v. informal* to annoy someone

[4]distort *v.* if someone distorts a sound, shape or character, it changes so that it is strange or unclear

[5]rank *v.* to have a position in a list of people who are put in order according to a quality

Comprehension Check

Which of the following statements are true according to Article 1? Check (✓) those statements.

_____ **1.** In the past, it was more common to have valedictorians.

_____ **2.** Today, competition for the role of valedictorian has increased.

_____ **3.** Taking music classes increases your chances of becoming a valedictorian.

Article 2

Preserve the Valedictorian Tradition
by Eric Effron

My memories of high school are fuzzy[1], but I do remember that our class valedictorian was Blaine Edell. Blaine was a modest, soft-spoken guy, but after being named first in the class, suddenly he was a star—touted[2] in the local papers, delivering the keynote speech at graduation. I thought of Blaine recently, when I read

5   that a growing number of school districts—from Toledo to Palm Beach, Fla., to Burlington, Vt.—are joining the movement to do away with valedictorians. Concerned that the "winner take all" valedictorian tradition breeds[3] unhealthy competition, many schools are either forgoing[4] the naming of a valedictorian altogether or giving the title to everyone who achieves a certain grade point average.

10   A Fairfax, Va., high school last year named 41 valedictorians. A school in Fresno, Calif., graduated 58 of them.

I'm sure they're all quite worthy. Still, with so many winners, something gets lost. After consulting with my kids, I can report that the high

15   school pecking order[5] hasn't evolved all that much over the years. The starting quarterback[6] is the big man on campus. The election for class president is essentially a popularity contest, and the prom king and queen[7] are not exactly picked

20   for their studiousness either. But as senior year draws to a close, the class starts to buzz[8] about the valedictorian contenders. And in the end, one student gets to bask in the limelight, cheered not for his charisma or athletic excellence,

25   but for being a superior . . . student. Do we really want to eliminate the one claim to high school

---

(continued)

fame based solely on academic achievement? After 30 years, I still remember
my class valedictorian; even now, the graduates in Fairfax or Fresno would be

29 | hard-pressed to name theirs.
_____
The Week. June 22, 2007. Reprinted with permission.

---

¹**fuzzy** *adj.* unclear

²**tout** *v.* to praise someone or something

³**breed** *v.* to cause a particular feeling or condition

⁴**forgo** *v.* decide not to do something

⁵**pecking order** *n.* the social system of a particular group of

people in which each one knows who is more important and less important than themselves

⁶**quarterback** *n.* the player in American football who directs the offense and throws the ball

⁷**prom king and queen** *n.* the two students who are

elected to be "royalty" at a formal dance for high school students

⁸**buzz** *n.* unofficial news or information that is spread by people telling each other

---

Comprehension Check

Which of the following statements are true according to Article 2? Check (✓) those statements.

_____ **1.** The author believes that the role of valedictorian is no longer meaningful and should be abolished.

_____ **2.** Some schools are choosing twenty or more valedictorians.

_____ **3.** Athletic excellence is part of being a valedictorian.

■ PRACTICE 3: Analyzing Arguments

The articles above have pro and con arguments for having valedictorians. Copy some of the most important arguments into the lists below. Be sure to put quotes around the sentences you copy. Also, put the last name of the author and the line number(s) of the quote in parentheses after the quote. (In this chapter, you'll use line numbers instead of page numbers for citations.)

Pro Valedictorians

1. *"With so many winners, something gets lost." (Effron, lines 12–13)* _____

2. _____

3. _____

4. _____

5. _____

Con Valedictorians

1. *"... the fight for the title has gotten out of hand." (DeCuir, line 8)*
    _____

2. _____

3. _____

4. _____

5. _____

Paraphrasing

Incorporating information from outside sources into your own writing makes it stronger. You can directly quote information from articles (as you learned in Chapter 5), or you can **paraphrase** it. Choosing to paraphrase a sentence instead of quoting it largely depends on the uniqueness of the sentence itself. If the sentence from the outside source is not expressed in any special way, and you only want to use the information, you should paraphrase it. To write a good paraphrase, you must:

- restate the sentence or passage in other words
- not change the meaning
- not leave out any essential information
- not add any information
- cite the source with an in-text citation

■ PRACTICE 4: Evaluating Paraphrases

Evaluate the paraphrases by comparing them to the original. Then circle the letter of the one that you think is best. Discuss your answers with a classmate.

1. *Original:* "Educators and students say pursuit of the top grade point average (GPA) has distorted the academic process" (DeCuir, 2007).

    a. Teachers and those they teach say that following the peak GPA has made the academic process unclear (DeCuir, 2007).

    b. According to teachers and students alike, the purpose of getting an education has been changed because students are only interested in getting the best GPA (DeCuir, 2007).

    c. Educators and students say following the best GPA has distorted the academic process (DeCuir, 2007).

2. *Original:* "Valedictorians have become less prominent at graduation ceremonies across the USA" (DeCuir, 2007).

    a. In the U.S., there have been fewer valedictorians speaking at graduation (DeCuir, 2007).

    b. At graduation ceremonies, valedictorians have become less famous in the United States of America (DeCuir, 2007).

    c. In the U.S., having a valedictorian speak at a graduation isn't as common these days as it has been in the past (DeCuir, 2007).

3. *Original:* "Concerned that the 'winner take all' valedictorian tradition breeds unhealthy competition, many schools are either forgoing the naming of a valedictorian altogether or giving the title to everyone who achieves a certain grade point average" (Effron, 2007).

    a. A large number of high schools are worried that the tradition of choosing a valedictorian makes students compete unreasonably with each other, so they are eliminating the honor or giving it to every A student (Effron, 2007).

    b. Because many schools are concerned that the valedictorian tradition is making students sick, they are eliminating valedictorians or making everyone a valedictorian (Effron, 2007).

    c. Eliminating valedictorians or giving the award to all straight-A students is becoming more common across the U.S.A. because students are becoming more competitive and winning everything (Effron, 2007).

■ PRACTICE 5: Analyzing the Model Essay

Do these tasks as you read the model essay.

1. Underline the four paraphrases and their citations in the model essay below. (For the purposes of this essay, line numbers are used instead of page numbers.)

2. Find the original sentences in the articles above and underline them.

3. Do the paraphrases support the arguments in the essay? Why or why not?

Model Essay

Valedictorian Nightmare

    Many high schools in the United States honor graduating students who have the highest grade point average by selecting them to be valedictorians. Being a valedictorian looks good on college applications, so students compete for this honor. However, the competition is becoming so intense at some schools that students are focusing too much on the end of high school and not on the years in high school themselves. In addition, their high school years are becoming so stressful that students are not able to enjoy them. Therefore, I think that the role of valedictorian in high school should be eliminated.

    First, students in high school should concentrate on learning in their classes and not on playing a big game with them. Students play games when they choose a class based on what the academic weight of the class is. For example, students may choose mathematics because it is worth more to their grade point average than an orchestra class is. In fact, as DeCuir reports, students may even decide to go to another school because they think that the other school will have easier classes (DeCuir, l. 18). With easier classes, they know they can get a better grade. Unfortunately, even parents get into the game. Nat Harrington gives the example of a student's mother asking for the requirements to be a valedictorian on the first day of school (DeCuir, l. 9–13). It seems that for these students and parents, finding ways to get a better GPA is more important than the actual learning that they are supposed to do in high school.

Secondly, having a valedictorian sets students up to see other students as the "enemy"—someone who wants to take something away from them. Some schools are worried that students may compete against each other in harmful ways in order to become the valedictorian (Effron, l. 7). There is already strong competition among students in sports; they don't need to compete in academic classes as well. In my view, students should be learning to cooperate in high school. By overstressing[1] the competition for valedictorian, schools are ignoring the importance of cooperation.

Third, students should be encouraged to take fine arts[2] classes to enrich[3] their high school experience. High school is perhaps the last time in their lives that many students can explore their aptitude[4] and interest in art and music. If students are worried that taking such a class will decrease the possibility of becoming valedictorian, they will miss this opportunity. As one student in Maryland said, the system is not reasonable. Her academic ranking fell because she took a music class (DeCuir, l. 24–25). She took the class, but it seems that she was being punished for taking it.

In conclusion, because the competition to become valedictorian encourages students to play a class-choosing game, sets students up to see one another as enemies instead of friends, and discourages enrollment in fine arts classes, I think that schools should abolish the valedictorian system. It may have been a true honor in the past, but nowadays, it has become a nightmare for any student wanting it.

> **What about you?**
>
> Do you think it is a good idea to have one valedictorian for a high school graduating class? Discuss your answer with a classmate.

[1] **overstress** v. to stress something or someone too much

[2] **fine arts** n. activities, such as painting and music, that are concerned with producing beautiful rather than useful things

[3] **enrich** v. to improve the quality of something, especially by adding things to it

[4] **aptitude** v. natural ability or skill, especially in learning

Guidelines for Paraphrasing

1. **Understand the Passage**

   Your first step to writing a paraphrase is to be sure that you understand the passage. If you do not understand the passage, you cannot evaluate the accuracy of your paraphrase, and you may confuse the reader or give false information.

2. **Change the Sentence Structure**

   Changing the sentence structure may be the most important skill in paraphrasing. When you maintain the same meaning using a different sentence type, you demonstrate that you fully understand the passage. There are three techniques for changing the sentence structure of a sentence.

   a. Changing Sentence Type

   As you know, there are three types of sentences: **simple**, **compound**, and **complex**. Changing from one type to another is a good way to paraphrase. The following sentence from Article 2 is a compound sentence because it combines two simple sentences with a coordinating conjunction.

   ➤ Blaine was a modest, soft-spoken guy, but after being named first in the class, suddenly he was a star—touted in the local papers.

   In this paraphrase of the sentence, you can see that the compound sentence has been changed to a complex sentence with an adverbial clause.

   ➤ **Although** Blaine was a shy, unassuming student, the hometown newspapers celebrated him once he became the valedictorian.

   The original could also change its sentence structure by using a transition instead of a coordinating conjunction.

   ➤ Blaine was a shy, humble student. **However**, once he became the valedictorian, the hometown newspapers celebrated him.

   b. Changing Phrases and Clauses

   Another technique to change a sentence is to change clauses into prepositional phrases and prepositional phrases into clauses. Here is the same paraphrase with a clause changed into a prepositional phrase.

   ➤ **Despite** Blaine's shyness and modesty, the hometown newspapers celebrated him once he became the valedictorian.

   c. Changing Sentence Voice

   Another paraphrasing technique is to change the voice from **active** to **passive** or vice versa.

   ➤ The hometown newspapers **celebrated** Blaine, a shy, humble student, once he became the valedictorian.

■ PRACTICE 6: Changing Sentence Structure

Below are simplified sentences from both articles on valedictorians. Rewrite each one by changing the sentence structure.

From Article 1

1. That's a positive development because the fight for the title has gotten out of hand.

2. Keely Breen dreamed of being her high school valedictorian. However, her high school made the decision to no longer name valedictorians at the end of Breen's junior year.

3. I went down this year because I took orchestra.

4. Sage Snider's academic ranking went down because she decided she wanted to take orchestra.

From Article 2

5. Blaine was a modest, soft-spoken guy, but after being named first in the class, suddenly he was a star.

6. After I consulted with my kids, I can report that the high school pecking order hasn't changed.

7. The election for class president is essentially a popularity contest, and the prom king and queen are not exactly picked for their studiousness.

8. I still remember my class valedictorian after 30 years; even now, the graduates in Fairfax or Fresno would be hard-pressed to name theirs.

3. Changing Words

   a. Using Synonyms

   The most obvious change you can make in a paraphrase is to change the individual words by using **synonyms**, words that have the same basic meaning. If you do not know a synonym, check a dictionary or a **thesaurus**, a book that lists synonyms instead of definitions. Most word-processing programs have thesauruses, and there are online thesauruses as well. However, you need to be cautious because one word may have several synonyms that have slightly different meanings. For example, look at the word "touted" in the second article:

   ➤ "... *touted** in the local papers . . ."

   Some synonyms from thesaurus.com* include *accustomed, acknowledged, allowed, arrived,* and *authorized.* The only one of these that would be acceptable in the context is *acknowledged.* Using any of the others would change the meaning.

---

*touted. (n.d.). *Roget's New Millennium™ Thesaurus, First Edition (v 1.3.1).* Retrieved November 02, 2007, from *http://thesaurus.reference.com/browse/touted.*

■ PRACTICE 7: **Choosing the Best Synonyms**

Below are possible synonyms for the other words in Article 2 on pages 91–92. First, find the word in the article and be sure that you understand the context. Then circle the best choice.

1. forgoing (line 8)
   a. give up   b. leave   c. quit
2. worthy (line 12)
   a. blameless   b. credible   c. deserving
3. buzz (line 21)
   a. report   b. rumor   c. scandal
4. contender (line 22)
   a. candidate   b. participant c. rival
5. charisma (line 24)
   a. charm   b. glamour   c. power

b. Changing the Type of Word

In addition to changing a word by using a synonym, you can also change the type of word. For example, in the following paraphrase from Article 1, the adjectives have been changed to a noun and a verb.

➤ Students may drop **enriching** courses in music or arts to grab advanced courses that have a higher **weighted** GPA.

➤ Students may want courses that have more academic **weight** in determining their GPA, so they transfer from music or art classes that are designed to **enrich** their academic classes.

■ PRACTICE 8: **Changing the Type of Word**

The sentences below are adapted from the articles on pages 90–92. In the paraphrases that follow, underline the word that has been changed and identify the type of change. Check your answers with a classmate.

1. Vermont's Burlington High School made the decision to no longer name valedictorians at the end of Breen's junior year.

   ➤ It was decided by Vermont's Burlington High School that the honor of valedictorian would no longer be given when Breen completed her third year.

2. Educators and students say pursuit of the top grade point average (GPA) has distorted the academic process.

   ➤ According to teachers and students alike, a distortion of the reason for an education occurs when students are only interested in getting the best GPA.

3. The valedictorian tradition causes unhealthy competition.

   ➤ It is not beneficial when students compete for the title of valedictorian.

4. One student is cheered not for his charisma or athletic excellence but for being a superior student.

   ➤ A high school honors one student not because he is charismatic or because he excels in sports but because he is an exceptional student.

Section Summary

In this section, you have learned several techniques in writing a paraphrase:

1. Changing sentence type
2. Changing clauses to phrases and vice versa
3. Changing sentence voice
4. Using synonyms
5. Changing word type

It is important to remember, however, that these techniques should be used in combination to write an acceptable paraphrase. Using just one or two does not change a sentence sufficiently to be considered a paraphrase.

■ PRACTICE 9: Paraphrasing Sentences

The sentences below are adapted from an article† by Lynn Thompson on the subject of valedictorians, published in the Seattle Times on June 15, 2005. Paraphrase each by using the techniques listed above. Then compare paraphrases with a classmate.

1. Skeptics say that so many students with perfect 4.0 GPAs is evidence of grade inflation; admirers say it's the product of smart, hard-working students at a school that encourages academic success.

2. Traditionally the highest-performing student, the valedictorian, gives the final address at graduation, but the increasing number of straight-A students has led some schools to abandon the award altogether.

3. Some national grading experts say that multiple valedictorians reflect a shift toward evaluating students based on mastery of course content, not in comparison to each other, as in the traditional bell curve system.

4. This year's valedictorians don't reflect the school's full diversity. Only one African-American student earned the top honor although blacks make up 22 percent of the student body.

---

†Copyright 2005, Seattle Times Company. Used with permission.

Avoiding Fragments

As you know, a simple sentence must have at least a subject and a verb with tense. If a string of words does not have these two basics, it is a **fragment**. Fragments should always be avoided in academic writing. Three common types of fragments are shown below. *X* = incorrect.

1. The verb with tense is missing.

    X Helena earning a top G.P.A.   (fragment)

    ➤ Helena was earning a top G.P.A.   (complete sentence)

2. The subject is missing.

    X Became the top student in his class.   (fragment)

    ➤ Juan became the top student in his class.   (complete sentence)

3. A dependent clause is punctuated as if it were an independent clause.

    X Because she was the valedictorian.   (fragment)

    ➤ Because she was the valedictorian, her resume
       made her stand out.   (complete sentence)

■ PRACTICE 10: **Identifying and Correcting Fragments**

*Write **C** in the blank if the sentence is complete. Write **F** if it contains a fragment, and correct it.*

_____ 1. The prom king and queen chosen by the entire class to be honored at the senior ball.

_____ 2. Katya wanted to take a piano class, but her parents wanted her to take biology.

_____ 3. When the graduation ceremony was over and the students had all gone home.

_____ 4. Even though Kim wanted to graduate with a perfect GPA, got one B in a math class.

_____ 5. Michelle did not go away to a big university because she didn't want to leave home.

_____ 6. Believed that he would get an athletic scholarship, so Chang-sun did not save money.

_____ 7. Joanna studying hard and struggling to get a passing grade in her English class.

_____ 8. While enrolling in classes, buying books and supplies, and looking for a part time job.

III LANGUAGE FOCUS

Parts of Speech

Traditionally, grammarians have identified eight **parts of speech**, or types of words: nouns, verbs, adjectives, adverbs, prepositions, pronouns, conjunctions, and interjections. For writing paraphrases, it is helpful to be familiar with the first four types. For example:

> ➤ **noun**   excellence
>
> ➤ **verb**   excel
>
> ➤ **adjective**   excellent
>
> ➤ **adverb**   excellently

■ PRACTICE 11: Reviewing Parts of Speech

Fill in the chart below with the missing parts of speech.

Noun	Verb	Adjective	Adverb
competition			
	cooperate		
		harmful	
			honorably
		intense	
	select		
studiousness			
			systematically

Changing Suffixes

Suffixes come at the end of a word and often show what part of speech it is. Knowing which suffixes go with which part of speech can be very helpful for writing a paraphrase. It is perhaps even more helpful to know what suffixes can be used to change from one type of word to another.

Study the chart on page 102. Try to come up with your own examples.

	Making Nouns		Making Verbs		Making Adjectives	
From Nouns	-cian	music → musician	-ate	elimination → eliminate	-al	nature → natural
					-fic	science → scientific
	-hood	sister → sisterhood	-ize	motor → motorize	-ful	joy → joyful
					-ic	academia → academic
	-ist	theory → theorist			-less	joy → joyless
					-y	worth → worthy
From Verbs	-ance	resist → resistance			-able	do → doable
	-ant	occupy → occupant			-ible	horrify → horrible
	-ee	employ → employee			-ive	cumulate → cumulative
	-ence	excel → excellence			-ous	study → studious
	-ment	achieve → achievement				
	-tion	compete → competition				
From Adjectives	-dom	free → freedom	-en	dark → darken		
	-ty	special → specialty				
	-ity	popular → popularity	-ify	beauty → beautify		
	-ness	dark → darkness				

■ *PRACTICE 12*: **Writing Sentences with Different Word Forms**

Rewrite each sentence using the given word. Both sentences must have the same meaning.

1. Kai studies a lot.

    studious   *Kai is very studious.*

2. As the sun set, the room became dark.

    darken _____

3. I can't do that task.

    doable _____

4. Faisal's excellence in math earned him a math scholarship.

    excel _____

5. Marie Claire occupies the corner office.

    occupant _____

6. The city council planned to make the city center more beautiful.

    beautify _____

IV WRITING TO COMMUNICATE

Your Turn

Write an essay in which you agree or disagree with this statement:

Generation Y‡ is not prepared to take on adult responsibilities because they have been too spoiled by their parents.

Paraphrase at least one sentence for each body paragraph from the following articles to support your opinion. Use citations that indicate the article and line number for each paraphrase. Write a References list on a separate page.

Article 3

I'm Just Sayin'

by Greg Sellnow

I received a news release the other day from a public relations firm, headlined "Are today's parents raising a generation of slackers[1]?" It was promoting a book by a guy named Terry Noble, who retired to a ranch in Montana at age 52 after selling the company he founded.

5   "They've been raised in an age of excess[2] consumption[3], where plastic surgery and flashy cars are given as high school graduation gifts," the news release begins. "Some experts say satisfying kids' self-esteem instead of teaching them about

---

(continued)

---

‡Generation Y: The generation born in the 1980s and 1990s, esp. in the U.S.

responsibility has left them poorly equipped to deal with adulthood. Armed with cell phones, laptops and their parents' cash, they have a sense of entitlement[4] like no

10 generation before them. Many have never rolled up their sleeves for physical labor or held a job . . .". It goes on to explain how Terry Noble was feeding 5,000 chickens by the time he was 9 and was operating his own crab boat by the time he was 14.

Please. I have two daughters in college now. One of them doesn't have a car, and the other one drives a 13-year-old Chevy Blazer that her grandparents gave her. One

15 daughter worked on campus in Ohio all summer and the other held down two jobs so she could pay for gas for the Blazer among other things. I don't know of a single teen-ager who's had plastic surgery, although my youngest daughter did add a second piercing to her ear a couple of weeks ago. (She paid for it herself.)

I take offense when people like Terry Noble, who is 62, say that all young people

20 are the same. Here's a reality check for Mr. Noble and others who claim their character was shaped and molded by manual labor.

Kids these days can succeed in life without having fed a single chicken, cleaned a single cow stall, or rebuilt the transmission of a single pickup. They can get just as far if they start out working in clothing stores, or caring for young children or watering the

25 fairways on a golf course.

Maybe I'm lucky, but the teenagers and young adults my children bring home are not spoiled brats[5] who never worked a day in their lives. They're nice kids whose parents are working hard to give them what they believe they deserve: a comfortable place to live, a good education, and a supportive home life while at the same time

30 expecting, and getting, something in return.

Post-Bulletin (Rochester, MN), September 8, 2007. Reprinted with permission.

---

[1]**slacker** *n.* someone who is lazy and does not do all the work they should

[2]**excess** *adj.* additional and more that is needed or allowed

[3]**consumption** *n.* the act of buying and using products

[4]**entitlement** *n.* the official right to have or receive something

[5]**spoiled brat** *n.* an impolite person, usually a child, who behaves badly because they are used to getting everything they want

Article 4

Not All Gen Y'ers are Spoiled Brats: What the Study on Narcissistic[1] Twentysomethings Really Reveals
by Sara Libby

A study led by San Diego psychologist Jean Twenge, released this week, found that today's college students are more narcissistic than ever—a development some fear will harm personal relationships and, ultimately, American society.

5 The researchers asked students questions on a "Narcissistic Personality Inventory," then compared the responses to those of college students in previous generations. Gen Y'ers agreed overwhelmingly with statements like "I think I am a special person" and "I can live my life any way I want to." The conclusion? My friends and I are an egotistical[2] bunch. The study has a point. We're the generation that always got a soccer trophy[3], no matter how well the team played—the ones whose precious

10 self-esteem has been pampered[4] and protected.

Now that we've come of age, it turns out we *are* pretty special. Older generations had to star in a movie or write a book to get the masses' attention. All we have to do is date six people at once and bam!—someone aims a camera at us. If that doesn't work, we can do the camera work ourselves and post the results on websites that begin with

15 words like "My" and "You," sites that also encourage us to share our favorite books, movies and TV shows simply because we're so damn interesting.

Naturally, all of this has given us a certain sense of entitlement, but I can't jump on board[5] with the study's suggestion that we're all just vain, spoiled brats. Plenty of college students commit themselves to noble[6] efforts, whether it's changing their

20 spring break vacation plans to help rebuild the Gulf Coast or signing up for programs like Teach for America. In the study, Twenge viewed this trend skeptically[7], suggesting that all charitable endeavors taken on by today's youth are done merely to make resumes look better.

Maybe that's true, but I think that instead of being monstrously more

25 self-centered than previous generations, we simply have the technological tools available to accommodate our self-absorbed tendencies, and we live in a world— not of our making—that considers self-esteem a prerequisite for success.

Still, if adults keep inflating[8] kids' egos without also teaching them the importance of working hard, valuing others and having character, then they'll reap

30 what they sow: kids who are treated like royalty—and act like it.

———

Los Angeles Times, March 2, 2007. Reprinted with permission.

[1]**narcissistic** *adj.* having a tendency to admire your own physical appearance or abilities

[2]**egotistical** *adj.* believing that you are better or much more important than other people

[3]**trophy** *n.* a prize for winning a race or other competition

[4]**pamper** *v.* to take care of someone kindly, sometimes too kindly

[5]**jump on board** *v.* to completely agree with or totally support something

[6]**noble** *adj.* morally good or generous in a way that should be admired

[7]**skeptically** *adv.* having doubts whether something is true, right, or good

[8]**inflate** *v.* to make something seem more important or impressive than it really is

Peer Help Worksheet

Use this peer help worksheet to help your classmate proofread his or her summary. For further instructions, refer to page 19.

CONTENT

1 Has the writer chosen one side of the issue? . . . . ❏

2 Is this point of view of the writer clearly stated in the thesis statement? . . . . ❏

3 Are the arguments in the body paragraphs clear? . . . . ❏

4 Do the arguments support the writer's opinion? . . . . ❏

5 Which of the articles are used as sources to support the writer's arguments? Check all that apply.

"Greg Sellnow: I'm just sayin'" . . . . ❏

"Not All Gen Y'ers Are Spoiled Brats" . . . . ❏

6 Does each body paragraph have at least one paraphrase? . . . . . ❏

ORGANIZATION

Is the organization of the essay clear? That is, does it clearly have:

1 an introductory paragraph? . . . . ❏

2 body paragraphs? . . . . ❏

3 a concluding paragraph? . . . . ❏

LANGUAGE

1 Are the writer's paraphrases written using his or her own words and grammar? . . . . ❏

2 Has the writer maintained the original meaning of the sentence? . . . . ❏

3 Are the authors of the articles correctly cited? . . . . ❏

4 Are the line numbers correct and correctly cited? . . . . ❏

5 Are there any fragments in the essay? . . . . ❏

Discuss any possible mistakes with the writer.

Writing to Communicate . . . More

As a journal entry or an in-class essay, choose a topic below. You can choose to focus on writing fluently, or you can practice any of the organizational techniques, sentence patterns, or language points discussed in this chapter. If you use a paraphrase from one of the articles used in this chapter, be sure to cite your paraphrase correctly.

1. What do you think of the role of valedictorian? Should it exist?
2. What are the advantages and disadvantages of being a member of a younger generation?
3. What are the differences between high schools in the United States and high schools in another country you are familiar with?
4. How is your schooling experience different from the schooling experience of your parents or grandparents?

I REVIEWING IDEAS

A. Evaluating Summaries

The box to the left contains an excerpt from Why Women Read More than Men *by Eric Weiner (posted on npr.org on September 5, 2007). The boxes on the right are summaries of the excerpt. Circle the number of the best summary. Be prepared to explain your choice to a classmate.*

Surveys consistently find that women read more books than men, especially fiction. Explanations abound, from the biological differences between the male and female brains, to the way that boys and girls are introduced to reading at a young age.

One thing is certain: Americans—of either gender—are reading fewer books today than in the past. A poll released last month by the Associated Press and Ipsos, a market-research firm, found that the typical American read only four books last year, and one in four adults read no books at all.

1.
There are many reasons that women read more than men, especially fiction, and Americans are reading less as well. The typical American read only four books last year.

2.
According to an article by Eric Weiner posted on npr.com ("Why Women Read More than Men"), surveys have found that men read less than women and that in general Americans are reading less than they used to.

3.
In "Why Women Read More than Men," Eric Weiner tries to explain why men don't read as much as women. He thinks it is because their brains are different and because of the way that boys and girls are taught to read. I agree with him.

B. Evaluating Paraphrases

Evaluate the paraphrases from the excerpt below taken from Think Pink—or at Least a Reddish Blue *by Benjamin Lester (ScienceNOW Daily News, 20 August 2007) by writing the letter of the mistake(s) listed on the line. Be prepared to explain your answer, to a classmate.*

Excerpt: Studies from as long ago as 1897 have hinted at differences in color preference between genders, suggesting that more females preferred reds than did males. But the data were murky and inconsistent, according to experts.

Mistakes: a. changed meaning

b. omitted important information

c. no citation or incomplete citation

d. used only one technique for paraphrasing

_____ 1. Studies from as long ago as 1897 have implied differences in color fondness between genders, signifying that more women favored reds than did men. However, the statistics were gloomy and incompatible, according to experts (Lester, 2007).

_____ 2. Experts from 1897 believed that there was a difference in the way that men and women see colors. They found that women liked red more than men did.

_____ 3. Differences in color preference between genders were hinted at by studies from as long ago as 1897. It was suggested that more females preferred reds than did males. But experts said that the data were murky and inconsistent.

_____ 4. According to Lester, the studies showed that men liked red more than women did, but they were unclear (2007).

II ERROR ANALYSIS

A. Sentence Structure

Find and correct the mistakes below. Check your answers with a classmate.

1. Before traveled to Scotland, Phillip read as many books about it as he could find.

2. Finishing her speech, the audience applauded the valedictorian enthusiastically.

3. Hoping for a baby girl but not wanting to disappoint her husband.

4. Because most women prefer pink to blue, girls' rooms pink instead of blue.

5. As their employers claim, that Generation Y is unprepared to lead.

B. Quotations, Citations, and References Lists

Check (✓) the correct item in each pair below. Be prepared to explain your choice to a classmate.

1. a quotation and its citation

   _____ "I have an inexplicable urge to find the old man," Palumbo writes, "a desperate need to thank him." (George, 2003)

   _____ "I have an inexplicable urge to find the old man," Palumbo writes, "a desperate need to thank him" (George, 2003).

2. an entry in a References list

   _____ Alder, J. (2007, December 24). The games of their lives. *Newsweek*, CL, 61.

   _____ Alder, Jerry. (2007, December 24). The games of their lives. *Newsweek*, CL, p. 61.

3. a paraphrase and its citation

   _____ Adding to the uncertainties parents feel about bringing up their children are the experts who have different opinions (Michelle Quinn, azcentral.com).

   _____ Adding to the uncertainties parents feel about bringing up their children are the experts who have different opinions (Quinn, 2004).

THE SHORT RESEARCH PAPER

THE FIRST DRAFT

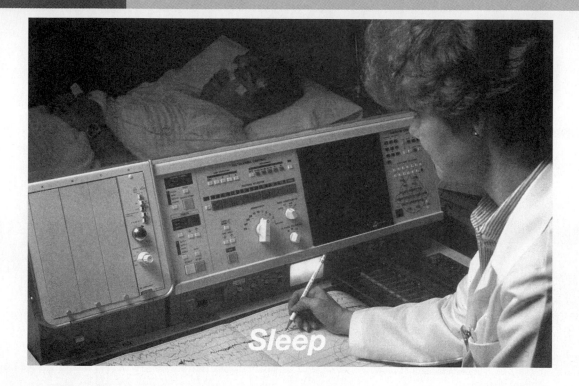

Sleep

WRITING FOCUS

The Short Research Paper

In university classes, you often write essays that include references to other sources that support your thesis statement and main ideas. To do that, you need to research what other people have said about your topic and incorporate relevant support from outside sources into your essay by summarizing, quoting, or paraphrasing it.

While you are going through the process of writing a short research paper, remember that no one else's words are as important as yours! As a writer, you use summaries, quotes, and paraphrases from others only to add weight to your arguments. Your professor wants to see that you have researched what others have said. However, the quality of your essay does not depend on how many references you have in your References list, but rather on how convincing your arguments are.

In this chapter, you will select a topic that you will continue to work with until the end of the term. Nevertheless, do not worry too much! You can change your topic if necessary. Writers do that all the time.

Understanding the Assignment

As you know, the first step in writing an essay is to understand the assignment. Here is the assignment from your English professor:

> Write a five-to-eight-page (1200–1800 words) research paper on a topic in your major that you want to explore further. The paper is due at the end of the semester and must include concrete support from two to four sources in the References list. Your paper must have one or two examples each of direct quotes, paraphrases, and summaries. Use APA formatting.

■ PRACTICE 1: Understanding the Assignment

To demonstrate that you understand the assignment, answer these questions. Then check your answers with a classmate.

1. What is the topic of the paper?

2. Why am I writing it?

3. Where does the information for the paper come from?

4. How long should it be?

5. When is it due?

6. How should I submit it?

Choosing a Topic

Think about a topic that is interesting to you and about which you have an opinion. Often the best type of academic writing occurs when you argue a position.

While there are hundreds of academic fields to study, it is common to organize them into three major categories: **hard sciences**, **social sciences**, and **arts and humanities**. The hard sciences are those where research can, at least to a certain degree, produce definitive results. The social sciences study the behavior of people and groups. Arts and humanities study the expression of the cultural aspects of people and groups.

Hard Sciences	Social Sciences	Arts and Humanities
biology	anthropology	the arts
chemistry	business management	communications
computer science	economics	history
engineering	law	language
mathematics	linguistics	literature
medicine	psychology	media studies
physics	sociology	philosophy

What about you?

Have you taken classes in any of the three categories listed? How did you like the classes? Share your answers with a classmate.

Narrowing Your Topic

After you have chosen a field of study, you will need to narrow it to a topic that is suitable for a five-to-eight page paper. For example, you could narrow sociology to human behavior and then narrow it further to the general topic of "sleep." This is a topic that you can brainstorm.

Brainstorming

As you remember, the purpose of brainstorming is to get out all the ideas that you can about your topic.

■ PRACTICE 2: Completing a Circle Diagram

The circle diagram below is partially filled in. With a classmate, fill in other ideas.

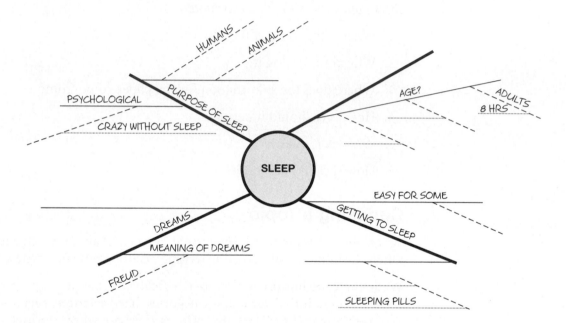

Writing a Working Thesis

After brainstorming, you should have several areas of interest from which to choose. At this point, you can further define your topic by writing a **working thesis**. It is called "working" because it probably will need refining as you research. Your research may even change your opinion about your topic. You are not tied down to an opinion at this point in the process.

However, you do need to start out with a point of view about a topic so you know how to direct your research. The circle diagram about "sleep" could contain four broad areas:

● purpose of sleep

● getting to sleep

● amount of sleep

● dreams

Look at the subcategories of each. Are there any possible topics that would have different points of view? Circle any and discuss your answers with a classmate.

You should have found that there are different points of view about, for example, "sleeping pills" and "the meaning of dreams," which could lead to a working thesis. Ask yourself these questions about each:

1. How much do I already know about this topic?
2. Do I have an opinion about it?
3. How interesting is it to me?

Perhaps you conclude that, while the meaning of dreams is interesting, you know more about sleeping pills. You also may already have a point of view about this topic given your experience and knowledge.

The first working thesis that you write can be relatively simple, with only a topic and a controlling idea. For example:

➤ Sleeping pills are dangerous.

With this working thesis, you are ready to begin your organization and research.

■ **PRACTICE 3: Writing Working Theses**

The broad topics below are from brainstorming sessions. Circle those that could lead to topics with two or more points of view. Then discuss with a classmate possible working theses that could develop from these topics.

1. types of cells
2. taxing items sold online
3. learning Sanskrit grammar
4. the causes of war
5. inventing the electron microscope
6. recent laws passed by the government
7. using stem cells for cancer research
8. stages of human development

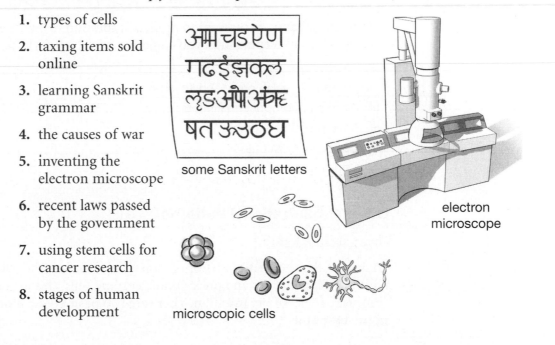

some Sanskrit letters

electron microscope

microscopic cells

Organizing Your Paper

After you have a working thesis, you can begin organizing your research paper. Organizing your ideas before you begin writing will help you:

1. organize your thoughts
2. show relationships between ideas
3. order your ideas logically
4. plan your research
5. write your first draft

Choosing an Organizational Pattern

Choose an organizational pattern that serves your topic and opinion. For example, in the first part of this book, you studied two organizational patterns: cause/effect and problem/solution. These patterns approach a topic quite differently. If your topic is sleeping pills and you want to discuss addiction to them, you could use one of the cause/effect patterns:

I. Introduction
II. Causes of addiction
III. Effects of addiction
IV. Conclusion

On the other hand, if you want to propose a solution to, say, the problem of getting to sleep without sleeping pills, you could use a problem/solution pattern:

I. Introduction with proposed solution
II. Benefits of proposed solution
III. Anticipated objections
IV. Counter-objections
V. Conclusion

Other Organizational Patterns

Comparison/Contrast

To discuss the similarities and/or contrasts between, say, the effectiveness of natural sleep remedies and prescription sleeping pills, choose a comparison/contrast pattern of organization. There are two basic styles: **block** and **point-by-point**.

Block	**Point-by-Point**
I. Introduction	I. Introduction
II. Natural sleep remedies	II. Point 1: Natural sleep remedies vs. sleeping pills
Point 1	III. Point 2: Natural sleep remedies vs. sleeping pills
Point 2	IV. Point 3: Natural sleep remedies vs. sleeping pills
Point 3	V. Conclusion
III. Sleeping pills compared to natural sleep remedies	
Point 1	
Point 2	
Point 3	
IV. Conclusion	

Persuasion

In a persuasive essay, you try to convince your reader with logical reasons. The reasons are usually presented individually in body paragraphs, which are ordered in one of two ways: **equal** or **least important to most important**. If, for example, you wanted to convince your reader of the dangers of sleeping pills, you could organize your essay in one of these ways:

Equal	**Least Important to Most Important**
I. Introduction	I. Introduction
II. Dangerous reason	II. Least dangerous reason
III. Dangerous reason	III. Next dangerous reason
IV. Dangerous reason	IV. Most dangerous reason
V. Conclusion	V. Conclusion

■ PRACTICE 4: Choosing an Organizational Pattern

*Decide which organizational pattern would lend itself to each topic below by writing **CE** (cause/effect), **PS** (problem/solution), **CC** (comparison/contrast), or **P** (persuasion). Note that more than one pattern is possible. When you are finished, discuss your answers with a classmate.*

_____ 1. caring for elderly parents   _____ 6. gender bias

_____ 2. child rearing   _____ 7. grading policies

_____ 3. climate change   _____ 8. means of transportation

_____ 4. feeding the poor   _____ 9. travel destinations

_____ 5. funding for a new museum   _____ 10. using animals in medical research

Making an Outline

Once you have chosen an organizational pattern, you can write your outline. Some professors will want you to turn in a formal outline along with your research paper, but often outlines are only for your eyes, to help with your own planning. Look at the example outline below. The writer has thought of some of the possible dangers of sleeping pills and used one for each body paragraph.

   I. Working thesis: Sleeping pills are dangerous.
  II. Reason 1: physical dependency
 III. Reason 2: psychological dependency
  IV. Reason 3: behavioral problems
   V. Reason 4: problems during daytime
  VI. Conclusion

This outline is very simple, and the writer certainly will add and subtract information as he or she learns more about the topic in the next phase of the process: research. For now, however, this **working outline** is enough to get started.

Writing the First Draft

It is a good idea to write your first draft before you begin your research. Remember that you research to find support for your ideas. By writing the first draft from your own ideas, you discover the areas that need support. This also prevents you from looking directly at an article while you write, which can lead to plagiarized passages.

This first draft is only for you. You will make many changes before you finish your final draft, so do not worry about grammar, punctuation, or spelling at this point. Also, you do not have to write it from beginning to end. Many writers find it useful to write the body paragraphs first, and later write the introductory paragraph and the concluding paragraph. You will probably want to unify each body paragraph with a clear topic sentence at this stage, though. However, there is no right or wrong procedure. You need to find a way that works for you.

In this first draft, the writer has identified some areas for research. Work with a classmate to identify other areas for research.

The Dangers of Sleeping Pills

A lot of people have trouble falling asleep at night. Some have trouble every night, *how many? get stats* and it affects their work the next day. Unfortunately, many people turn to sleeping pills to help them fall asleep. But, sleeping pills are dangerous.

all sleeping pills? find types

The first danger is that sleeping pills can cause physical dependency. Most sleeping pills are designed to be taken for a short period, so when people take them long term, their body gets used to having them. Then, it becomes impossible for them to fall asleep without sleeping pills. When they try, they experience headaches, become anxious and restless, and even suffer from insomnia.

In addition to physical dependency, sleeping pills can also cause psychological dependency. Users who believe that they can't get to sleep without the drug often can't. It becomes a vicious cycle. *need more info about this*

The third danger is that it can lead to dangerous behavior while sleeping. I read an article about how a woman who had taken a sleeping pill woke up and found a lot of candy bar wrappers on her bed. She didn't remember eating them, but she must have. The same article talked about people driving cars while sleeping! And they didn't remember until they woke up in their pajamas on the side of the road with a policeman. This obviously is a huge danger, not only to the driver but also to the other drivers and pedestrians on the road.

The last danger is that people have problems the day after taking a sleeping pill. The purpose of sleep is, after all, to allow you to work the next day, so when a sleeping pill prevents this, there is no reason to take it. Many sleeping pills are sedatives and these take a long time to pass out of your system. If you don't sleep long enough to allow this to happen, you may go to work the next day

---

(continued)

with sedatives in your system. You may feel drowsy and sleepy all day, and this may make it difficult to concentrate on what you are doing!

In short, people shouldn't take sleeping pills because they can cause physical and psychological addiction. They can also make you do crazy things while sleeping. Most importantly, though, they don't help and may make you feel tired the next day. People should try other methods of getting to sleep instead.

II SENTENCE FOCUS

Avoiding Bias in Your Writing

In all of your academic writing, it is important to use **unbiased** language. That is, you must avoid using terms that could offend anyone who is reading your paper. Most of the changes you may make will be minor vocabulary differences, but the impact of not making these changes can be huge.

Avoiding "Labeling" Language

The first rule in avoiding bias in English is to only refer to a person's race, ethnicity, disability, or age if it is necessary to the content of your essay. In other words, write as though there are no differences among people. For example, instead of saying "a white person" or "a black person" or "a disabled person," simply write "a person."

Of course, sometimes it is necessary to designate a person's race or ethnicity. In this case, it is important to use a term that is acceptable to that specific group of people. Usually terms like "Chinese American," "Korean American," "Mexican American," and "Cuban American" are acceptable. Native Americans, however, often prefer to be called by their tribe's name, such as "Navajo" or "Hopi." The term "blacks" (with or without a capital letter) is also acceptable, but many prefer the term "African American." The term "white" is the most commonly used word to refer to people of European ancestry.

In addition to race, you may need to comment on a person's physical or mental impairment. In these situations, use the term "disabled" instead of "handicapped" because "disabled" refers to a person's attributes, and a "handicap" refers to the activity that a person cannot do because of a disability. For example, a person who is blind can still learn to play the violin. The person is disabled, but not handicapped.

Avoiding Sexist Language

One problem that arises when people write in English is the use of the singular, third-person pronouns (*he*, *his*, *him*) to refer to a person of unknown gender. For example:

➤ When <u>a student</u> arrives late, **he** interrupts the class.

In times past, using "he" as a general pronoun for any human wasn't considered a problem, but nowadays, it is seen as sexist. Writers have gotten around this by using "he/she," "he or she," and even "s/he," but these are not considered practical alternatives. A better way to avoid this problem is to use plural nouns for people in general. For example:

➤ When <u>students</u> arrive late, ***they*** interrupt the class.

This solution almost always works and is preferable to the other options.

Another problem with sexist language concerns the names of common professions. For example:

➤ The <u>fireman</u> saved the girl.

In the past, all people who worked for the fire department were men, but these days, there are many women as well. The language needs to reflect this.

➤ The <u>firefighter</u> saved the girl.

Other common professions and their unbiased counterparts are listed below.

businessman	businessperson
chairman	chair or chairperson
congressman	representative or senator
fireman	firefighter
mailman	mail carrier or postal worker
policeman	police officer
saleswoman or salesman	salesclerk
steward or stewardess	flight attendant
waiter or waitress	server

■ PRACTICE 6: Rewriting Sentences with Biased Language

Each of the sentences below has biased language in it. Rewrite it so that it is more acceptable in an academic paper. There may be more than one instance of biased language in one sentence. Work with a classmate.

1. The old black man who lives next to me gave a very eloquent speech at the town hall meeting.

2. It's important that any student cafeteria worker cover his hair with a net.

3. The chairman of the French club must be able to speak French.

4. Nadia, who is in a wheelchair, wrote an excellent term paper.

5. There is an organization for handicapped people on campus. It is open to any person who thinks he needs assistance.

6. Sometimes the mailman is late, so a student has to wait for his mail.

7. The Vietnamese winner of the lottery said that he was going to buy a new house for his mother.

8. Nowadays, policemen need to attend classes on avoiding racial profiling.

Commonly Confused Words: Adjectives and Adverbs

Both native and non-native speakers confuse the pairs of words below. Study the definitions and sample sentences to understand the difference between the two words in each pair.

1. **conscious** *adj.* awake and able to understand what is happening around you

   conscience *n.* the part of your mind that tells you the difference between right and wrong

   ➤ During the last rainstorm, I witnessed a bad car accident in which a person was thrown from the car. I could see that she was not <u>conscious</u>. I wanted to leave her there, but my <u>conscience</u> would not allow it. I waited until the ambulance arrived.

2. **further** *adj.* more or to a greater degree; used to talk about time, quantities, or degrees

   farther *adj.* the comparative form of "far;" used to talk about distance

   ➤ We need to do <u>further</u> research about the distance between Los Angeles and San Diego. It may be <u>farther</u> than we think it is.

3. **economic** *adj.* relating to trade, industry, and the management of money

   economical *adj.* using money, time, or goods carefully without wasting them

   ➤ The company's president said, "We're in a difficult <u>economic</u> situation because of the bad weather last winter. We must be <u>economical</u> about every cent that we spend."

4. **hardly** *adv.* almost not

   hard *adv.* using a lot of effort, energy, or attention

   ➤ I <u>hardly</u> knew what to say. I had worked so <u>hard</u> on finishing the project on time, and then I found out it was no longer needed.

5. **maybe** *adv.* a sentence adverb to say that something may happen or may be true, but you are not certain

   may be *modal and v.* indicating possibility or permission

   ➤ <u>Maybe</u> I'll recognize him when I see him, but he <u>may be</u> very different now.

6. **than** *conj.* used when comparing two things

   then *adv.* after something has happened

   ➤ We need to wake up earlier <u>than</u> we did yesterday. <u>Then</u> we need to shower before our guests get up.

■ PRACTICE 7: Choosing the Correct Word

Circle the correct word to go in each blank. Then compare your answers with a classmate.

Shopping for a New Mattress

My wife and I encountered two totally different types of salesclerks when we went shopping for a new mattress last weekend. We were
_____ inside the store when the first salesclerk came running
(1. hard / hardly)
up to us. She took us immediately to the best mattress in the store. It was
comfortable, but it was too expensive. _____ one day we'll
(2. May be / Maybe)
win the lottery. _____ we can buy that bed, but our
(3. Than / Then)
_____ situation does not allow us to now. It almost cost more
(4. economic / economical)
_____ our new car! She tried _____ to get us to buy
(5. than / then)   (6. hard / hardly)
the bed even as we were walking out the door. We walked a little
_____ down the block and found another store. The salesclerk in
(7. farther / further)
the second store was much calmer. In fact, he left us alone completely, and
when we finally found an _____ mattress and wanted to buy it, he
(8. economic / economical)
was _____ _____! We literally had to wake him up in
(9. hard / hardly)   (10. conscious / conscience)
order to sell us the mattress. As we loaded the mattress into our truck, we
thought that there _____ a happy medium between these two
(11. may be / maybe)
types of clerk, but we certainly hadn't met one that day.

What about you?

Have you ever had a particularly easy or difficult time shopping for something? Tell your classmate about it.

Your Turn

Follow the steps below in order to write your own working thesis.

1. Check (✓) the boxes that apply to you.

   a. What general field of study interests you?

   ❏ Hard sciences   ❏ Social sciences   ❏ Arts and Humanities

   b. In the general field that you chose, which area interests you the most?

Hard Sciences		Social Sciences		Arts and Humanities	
Biology	❏	Anthropology	❏	Communications	❏
Chemistry	❏	Business	❏	Dance	❏
Computer science	❏	Economics	❏	Drama	❏
Engineering	❏	Law	❏	Foreign languages (Which one? _____)	❏
Mathematics	❏	Linguistics	❏	History	❏
Medicine	❏	Psychology	❏	Literature	❏
Physics	❏	Sociology	❏	Media studies	❏
Other: _____		Other: _____		Music	❏
				Philosophy	❏
				Studio art	❏
				Other: _____	

2. On another piece of paper, brainstorm your topic by drawing a circle diagram. Then show your diagram to a classmate. Together, add some more ideas.

3. Look again at the circle diagram on your topic. To write your working thesis, follow these steps:

   a. Circle the subcategories that may have different points of view.

   b. Ask yourself about each subcategory that you circled:

      i. How much do I already know about this topic?

      ii. Do I have an opinion about it?

      iii. How interesting do I find it?

   c. Choose one that you already have an opinion about.

   d. Write a simple working thesis with a topic and controlling idea.

4. Choose an appropriate organizational pattern for your topic and working thesis statement. Review the patterns on pages 116–117.

5. Write a short outline based on what you already know about your topic.

6. Write your first draft from the outline. Do not worry about grammar, punctuation, or spelling. Write unified body paragraphs with topic sentences. Then write your introductory and concluding paragraphs.

7. Reread your essay and identify areas for research.

Peer Help Worksheet

Use this peer help worksheet to help you give feedback to a classmate about the first draft. For further instructions, refer to page 19.

CONTENT

1 Does the working thesis have a point of view? . . . . ❑

2 Do the points in the body paragraphs support the thesis statement? . . . . ❑

3 Are there any other areas of research that you can suggest? . . . . . ❑

ORGANIZATION

1 Does the working thesis have a topic and a controlling idea? . . . . ❑

2 Has the writer chosen an appropriate organizational pattern for the topic? . . . . ❑

3 Do all the body paragraphs have topic sentences? . . . . ❑

LANGUAGE

1 Has the writer avoided biased language? . . . . ❑

2 If the writer has used any of the commonly confused words, has he or she used them correctly? . . . . ❑

If not, discuss any possible mistakes with the writer.

Writing to Communicate . . . More

As a journal entry or an in-class essay, choose a topic below to practice one of the new organizational patterns discussed in this chapter.

1. Compare/contrast the sleep patterns and habits of two people you know. Whose lifestyle is healthiest?

2. Imagine that you have a friend that is addicted to sleeping pills. What would you say to persuade him or her to stop using them?

3. What are some causes of insomnia (sleeplessness)? What are some effects? What are some solutions?

Sleeping Pills

I WRITING FOCUS

What about you?

When you want to find information quickly, where do you look? Share your answer with a classmate.

Now that you have written the first draft of your research paper, and you have an idea of what areas of research you need to concentrate on, you are ready to begin your research.

Concrete Support

Concrete support is information from outside sources, such as books, articles, and Web sites, that you insert into your essay to strengthen your arguments. Using concrete support makes the ideas in your essay more convincing by adding facts, statistics, and expert opinions.

Finding Concrete Support

Concrete support can be found in periodicals, such as newspapers, magazines, and journals at a public library or a university library. Many magazines and the bigger newspapers also keep back issues, or selected articles from those issues, on their Web sites. However, not all articles from the archives of the bigger newspapers are free to read online, so you might need to read them at a library. You also need to discover which magazines and journals publish articles about the topic you are interested in. That means searching the library's databases. If you go to a library and ask the reference librarian, he or she will gladly help you start searching in the best database for your topic.

You can also find concrete support on the World Wide Web by using a virtual library to search for books or periodicals or by using a public search engine to find online articles and Web sites. You can also search, for example, the United States Library of Congress (http://www.loc.gov) or the California Digital Library (http://www.cdlib.org/). Some popular public search engines are http://www.google.com, http://www.yahoo.com, and http://www.ask.com.

When you find a source, make a copy of it. Many professors want you to turn in copies of all the articles from which you cite passages. Then, when you are reading an article and find a piece of concrete support that you may want to use, copy the support on a small note card. On the back of the card, copy all the information needed for your References list. Using note cards in this way allows you later to categorize them according to the points they support. When you are ready to write your References list, all the information you need is in one place.

Guidelines for Choosing a Piece of Concrete Support

1. Carefully consider the source
   a. Newspapers: Use well known ones, such as *The New York Times, Los Angeles Times,* or *Chicago Tribune.* Online versions of these newspapers are the same as the hard copies.
   b. Magazines: Use well known ones, such as *Time, U.S. News and World Report,* and *Newsweek.* Online versions of these magazines are the same as the hard copies.
   c. Journals: Academic journals are credible, but they may be very technical. Online versions of these journals are the same as the hard copies.
   d. Web sites: Be extra critical and skeptical about the credibility of documents that you find on the Web. Ask yourself these questions:
      i. What is the source? If you cannot find it, do not use the site.
      ii. If you can find the source, is it trustworthy?
         1. University publications are usually trustworthy.
         2. Government documents may or may not be.
         3. Blogs, which are free, written discussions of various topics, are not always reliable. Make sure the author is an expert in the field before using his or her opinions.
2. In general, do not use information that is older than five years.
3. Choose a passage that directly supports your point.
4. Do not take a passage out of context.
5. Do not use more than two pieces of concrete support in one paragraph. Most of the paragraph should be your own words.
6. Do not choose a passage that is too technical or field-specific for your reader to understand.

■ PRACTICE 1: Evaluating Research Results

Read the description of each piece of concrete support below. Decide whether it would be appropriate to use in a research paper. Discuss your answers with a classmate.

1. An encyclopedia article about human behavior from a 2001 volume

2. A *Los Angeles Times* editorial endorsing a presidential candidate

3. An article from a tabloid newspaper that you bought at a supermarket

4. A blog by a respected *New York Times* reporter

5. A reader's response to the blog by the reporter

6. An article from Stanford University's online *Encyclopedia of Philosophy* called "The Philosophy of Neuroscience" dated January 24, 2006

7. A quote from an article on the Mayo Clinic's Web site

8. An advertisement for a product that you are researching

Inserting Concrete Support into Your Essay

There are three ways of incorporating concrete support into your paper: by **summarizing**, **quoting**, and **paraphrasing**. Briefly, summarizing (discussed in Chapter 4) is writing the main ideas of something you have read in your own words, quoting (discussed in Chapter 5) is directly copying an excerpt from a text, and paraphrasing (discussed in Chapter 6) is writing the same information in different words.

Deciding which way to use concrete support can be difficult, but there are some guidelines that you can follow:

Summarize when . . .	Quote when . . .	Paraphrase when . . .
• the main points of the passage or article are enough to support your ideas	• the original words are special or unique • the quote will have a greater impact in your paper • you want to prove that the person you are quoting actually made the statement	• passages are 1-3 sentences long • the complete passage is relevant to your point • the information is more important than the way in which the idea is expressed

■ PRACTICE 2: Deciding to Quote, Paraphrase, or Summarize

Below are descriptions of pieces of concrete support for a paper. With a classmate, discuss which form you would use to place each piece into your paper.

1. a two-page article that highlights five major points

2. This sentence that Princess Diana said about land mines: "The world, with its many other preoccupations, remains largely unmoved by a death roll of something like 800 people every month—many of them women and children."

3. a description of a biological process

4. This sentence that Mahatma Gandhi said: "Where there is love there is life."

5. a popular blog by someone whose qualifications aren't on his site

6. This sentence from an article by Patricia Corrigan, a writer for the *St. Louis Post-Dispatch*: "For years, sleep experts have recommended that adults get at least eight hours of sleep a night to function properly."

7. This Afghani proverb: No one says his own buttermilk is sour.

8. the conclusion of a scientific experiment

■ PRACTICE 3: Inserting Appropriate Support into the First Draft

Below are two body paragraphs of the first draft of the essay on sleeping pills and five note cards with pieces of concrete support. Work with a classmate on the following tasks:

1. Decide if each piece of support is relevant.
2. If it is, decide where in the essay it should go.
3. Discuss whether you would summarize, quote, or paraphrase it.

> The third danger is that it can lead to dangerous behavior while sleeping. I read an article about how a woman who had taken a sleeping pill woke up and found a lot of candy bar wrappers on her bed. She didn't remember eating them, but she must have. The same article talked about people driving cars while sleeping! And they didn't remember until they woke up in their pajamas on the side of the road with a policeman. This obviously is a huge danger, not only to the driver but also to the other drivers and pedestrians on the road.

The last danger is that people have problems the day after taking a sleeping pill. The purpose of sleep is, after all, to allow you to work the next day, so when a sleeping pill prevents this, there is no reason to take it. Many sleeping pills are sedatives, and these take a long time to get out of your system. If you don't sleep long enough to allow this to happen, you may go to work the next day with sedatives in your system. You may feel drowsy and sleepy all day, and this may make it difficult to concentrate on what you are doing!

a.

Saul, Stephanie "FDA Warns of Sleeping Pills' Strange Effects" The New York Times (March 15, 2007)

Sleep-drivers reported frightening episodes in which they recalled going to bed, but woke up to find they had been arrested roadside in their underwear or night-clothes. The agency said that it was not aware of any deaths caused by sleep-driving.

b.

Saul, Stephanie "FDA Warns of Sleeping Pills' Strange Effects" The New York Times (March 15, 2007)

Some of the patients gained weight before discovering that they were getting up at night to cook and eat.

c.

Saul, Stephanie "FDA Warns of Sleeping Pills' Strange Effects" The New York Times (March 15, 2007)

Use of those medications and other similar drugs has soared by more than 60 percent since 2000, fueled by television, print and other advertising. Last year, makers of sleeping pills spent more than $600 million on advertising aimed at consumers.

d.

"Study: Sleep deficit may be impossible to make up" USA Today (November 27, 2007)

New research suggests an added risk to losing sleep day after day: Humans and animals that have chronic sleep deprivation might reach a point at which the very ability to catch up on lost sleep is damaged, says Fred Turek, a sleep researcher at Northwestern University in Evanston, Ill.

e.

"Side Effects of Sleeping Pills" Apollo Health (2007)

While defending the use of sleeping pills, pharmaceutical companies counter that most of the people who use sleeping pills take them for a few weeks or less. What they don't say, however, is that the vast majority of all prescriptions are repeat prescriptions to chronic insomniacs.

Avoiding Faulty Parallelism

In addition to good organization and support in your writing, your sentences should be well written and error-free. Making sure that sentences with coordinating conjunctions and correlative conjunctions have good parallel structure is part of writing good sentences.

Good parallelism in sentences requires that the grammatical structures on either side of a coordinating conjunction be the same. For example:

➤ <u>Getting to sleep</u>, <u>staying asleep</u>, **and** <u>waking up refreshed</u> are the ideals
    gerund phrase   gerund phrase   gerund phrase

for a good night's sleep.

➤ You can use <u>herbal tea</u>, <u>melatonin</u>, **or** <u>sleeping pills</u> to help you get to
            noun   noun   noun

sleep.

Structures also need to be parallel in sentences with correlative conjunctions. There are four of these types of conjunction: *both . . . and, not only . . . but also, either . . . or*, and *neither . . . nor*. With these conjunctions, what comes between the two parts has to be the same as what comes after. For example:

➤ You can buy melatonin **both** <u>at a pharmacy</u> **and** <u>at a supermarket</u>.
                         prep. phrase   prep. phrase

➤ **Either** <u>you should go to bed earlier</u>, **or** <u>you should sleep later</u>.
          sentence   sentence

➤ You should **neither** <u>drink</u> **nor** <u>eat</u> anything with caffeine before bed.
                  verb   verb

➤ **Not only** <u>herbal teas</u> **but also** <u>melatonin</u> is sold over the counter.
          noun   noun

■ **PRACTICE 4: Correcting Faulty Grammatical Structures**

Identify and correct the errors in grammatical structures in the following sentences. Check your answers with a classmate.

1. Sleep specialists recommend both getting up at the same time and you should go to bed at the same time every day.

2. Either chamomile tea or drinking passion fruit tea can help you fall asleep.

3. Antihistamines relieve the symptoms for not only colds but also for allergies.

4. You should watch for feelings of anxiety, abnormal thinking, and you might get amnesia while taking this sleeping pill.

5. Taking sleeping pills for a short amount of time is neither harmful nor is it addictive.

6. You should see either your doctor or you should see a specialist about your sleeping problems.

7. Antihistamines can make you drowsy both after you take them and the next morning.

Subject/Verb Agreement and Correlative Conjunctions

1. Since *both . . . and* always indicates two items, the verb has to be plural.

   ➤ **Both** pharmacies **and** supermarkets <u>sell</u> melatonin.

2. With *either . . . or*, *neither . . . nor*, and *not only . . . but also* the verb should agree with the subject following the second part of the correlative conjunction.

   ➤ **Either** herbal teas **or** melatonin <u>is</u> natural.

   ➤ **Either** melatonin **or** herbal teas <u>are</u> natural.

   ➤ **Neither** my sisters **nor** my brother <u>has</u> trouble sleeping.

   ➤ **Neither** my brother **nor** my sisters <u>have</u> trouble sleeping.

   ➤ **Not only** the newspapers **but also** the magazine <u>has</u> articles about sleep aids.

   ➤ **Not only** the magazine **but also** the newspapers <u>have</u> articles about sleep aids.

Word Order and Correlative Conjunctions

When the parallel structures are clauses, you must use question word order after the negative parts of correlative conjunctions (*not only, neither, nor*).

   ➤ **Neither** <u>can Lucy get up</u> early **nor** <u>can she stay</u> up late.

   ➤ **Not only** <u>do sleep specialists recommend</u> antihistamines, but they also recommend melatonin.

■ PRACTICE 5: Correcting Faulty Parallelism

*Write **C** in the blank if the sentence is correct, and write **I** if it is incorrect. Then correct the incorrect sentences. Check your answers with a classmate.*

_____ 1. I like neither chamomile tea nor passion fruit tea.

_____ 2. Not only I have trouble sleeping, but also my husband does.

_____ 3. Both our old mattresses and our new one isn't very comfortable.

_____ 4. You can look online for a drugstore, or can you look in the telephone book.

_____ 5. You can either choose to run or to walk in the marathon.

_____ 6. Most people neither suffer side effects, nor do they become addicted to sleeping pills.

_____ 7. Early to bed and early to rise makes you healthy, wealthy, and wise.

_____ 8. Neither sleep eating nor sleep driving sound possible, but many people have reported such activities.

Verbs of Urgency

Often when you are writing a persuasive essay, you want to make a strong statement. You can show your strong feelings with a **verb of urgency** in the main clause of a complex sentence with a noun clause. Then, in the noun clause, use the simple form of the verb (with no agreement or tense). For example:

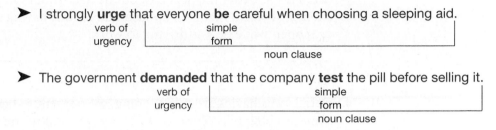

➤ I strongly **urge** that everyone **be** careful when choosing a sleeping aid.

➤ The government **demanded** that the company **test** the pill before selling it.

Other verbs of urgency include *advise, ask, desire, insist, recommend, suggest,* and *request.*

Adjectives of Urgency

There is also a group of adjectives that require the use of the simple form of the verb in sentences that follow this pattern:

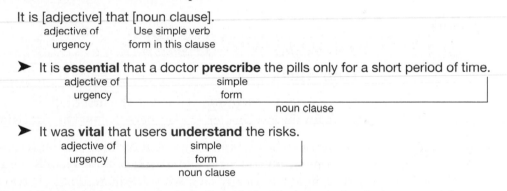

It is [adjective] that [noun clause].

➤ It is **essential** that a doctor **prescribe** the pills only for a short period of time.

➤ It was **vital** that users **understand** the risks.

Other adjectives of urgency include *best, desirable, imperative, important,* and *urgent.*

■ PRACTICE 6: Using Verbs and Adjectives of Urgency

For each situation below, write one sentence using a verb of urgency and one sentence using an adjective of urgency. Compare your sentences with a classmate.

1. Delilah was having a difficult time completing the project her boss had given her at work, so she was staying up later each night by drinking lots of coffee. She finally finished the project, but then she was having difficulty falling asleep even though she had stopped drinking coffee at night.

   Delilah should have asked that she be given more time for the project.

   It is essential that Delilah get some sleep!

2. I have been taking sleeping pills for about ten months. I want to stop, but every time I try, I feel so depressed, confused, and anxious. Furthermore, my insomnia is worse than ever. I usually end up taking a pill anyway because I know I have to go to work the next day.

_____

_____

3. Peter had a terrible cold, so he took some antihistamines before he went to bed. He felt better the next day, but he had trouble staying awake at work. After the second night, he noticed that he was having a hard time keeping his eyes open while he was driving to work.

_____

_____

4. Zorana was having trouble sleeping, so she went to her doctor to get some sleeping pills. They worked very well, but in the morning, she noticed that there were crumbs in her bed. She wondered why her husband had been eating in bed. The next morning, she found an apple core and half a carrot in her bed. She knew it couldn't be her husband's because he was out of town.

_____

_____

IV WRITING TO COMMUNICATE

Your Turn

Now it is your turn to add support to the first draft of your research paper that you wrote for the last chapter's assignment. Follow this procedure:

1. Review the original assignment for information regarding the types and amount of concrete support you can use. Here is the assignment again. The assignment clearly says that you will need at least two sources but that you can not use more than four. You should probably find six or seven sources.

> Write a five-to-eight-page (1200-1800 words) research paper on a topic in your major that you want to explore further. The paper is due at the end of the semester and must include concrete support from two to four sources in the References list. Your paper must have one or two examples each of direct quotes, paraphrases, and summaries. Use APA formatting.

2. Find some sources at the library and/or online. Make copies of all the articles that you think you might use. Be sure that the copies have all the information you will need to cite them and list them in your References list (see Chapter 5). During your research, you may come across information that causes you to rethink your position or refocus your paper. This is part of the research process, so do not hesitate to change your paper if necessary. If you make a change, go through the processes described in Chapter 7 again:

   a. Write a working thesis.

   b. Write an outline.

   c. Write a first draft without looking at the sources.

3. Once you find some sources, look carefully for passages that support the points in your paper. Check the assignment again to remind yourself of its details. For this particular assignment, you need to have at least one summary, one quote, and one paraphrase, but you cannot have more than two of each. Review the basics for each of these forms:

   a. Summarize a passage because it has the main ideas that support your points.

   b. Quote a passage because of its uniqueness and eloquence.

   c. Paraphrase a passage because it is only one or two sentences long and it directly supports your point.

4. Once you have chosen the passages and written your summaries and paraphrases, write another draft of your paper with the concrete support inserted. Put an in-text citation at the end of each piece of support.

5. Make a References list.

Peer Help Worksheet

Use this peer help worksheet to help you give feedback to a classmate about his or her second draft. For further instructions, refer to page 19.

CONTENT

1 Do the pieces of concrete support that the writer has chosen support the arguments that he or she is making? . . . .❑

2 What type of concrete support has the writer used?

(Check all that apply)

One or two summaries . . . .❑

One or two quotations . . . .❑

One or two paraphrases . . . .❑

3 Do all the entries in the References list seem well chosen? . . . . . .❑

ORGANIZATION

1 Does the thesis statement need a predictor? . . . .❑

2 Does the writer have an effective hook in the introduction? . . . . . .❑

3 Is there a smooth transition from the hook to the thesis statement? . . . .❑

LANGUAGE

1 Has the writer avoided using faulty parallelism? . . . .❑

2 Has the writer used any verbs or adjectives of urgency correctly? . . . .❑

3 Are the in-text citations formatted correctly? . . . .❑

4 Is the References list formatted correctly? . . . .❑

If not, discuss any possible mistakes with the writer.

Writing to Communicate . . . More

As a journal entry or an in-class essay, choose a topic below. You can choose to focus on writing fluently, or you can practice any of the organizational techniques, sentence patterns, or language points discussed in this chapter.

1. Write a short summary/response to one of the articles that you found about your topic. See Chapter 4 to review the elements of such an assignment. Submit the article along with your summary.

2. Paraphrase the sentences below taken from an article[1] used for the research paper in this chapter.

   a. Although the agency says that problems with the drugs are rare, reports of the unusual side effects have grown as use of sleeping pills has increased.

   b. In each case the consumers had no recollection of the events, which they said had occurred after they took their pills and headed for bed.

   c. An agency official said yesterday that the activities associated with the drugs went beyond mere sleepwalking.

   d. Besides warning against alcohol use, the new labels and guides will tell consumers that they should not take the pills with other drugs that suppress the nervous system.

---

[1]Saul, S. (2007, March 15). U.S. calls for strong warnings on sleep aids' strange effects. *The New York Times* p. A.1.

CHAPTER 9

REVISING AND EDITING

The Dangers of Sleeping Pills

I | WRITING FOCUS

Revising and editing is the last step to the process of writing a research paper. Before you begin this step, it is a good idea to take a break from the process if time allows. This way, you will be able to look at your essay from a more objective point of view.

What about you?

Share any concerns you have about the organization of your paper with a classmate.

Revising

You should always revise your essay for organization and content before you edit it for grammar, language, and format since your revisions may eliminate some of the editing that you have to do.

Checking the Organization

Reread your essay carefully, concentrating on these areas:

1. Your introductory paragraph
   a. Does it have a hook that grabs the reader's attention?
   b. Is there a transition from your hook to your thesis statement?
   c. Is the thesis statement placed at the end of the introduction?
   d. Is the thesis statement the main idea of your paper?

2. Your body paragraphs

   a. Is each paragraph well organized with a topic sentence and supporting sentences?

   b. Are there transitions between the body paragraphs?

3. The order of your ideas

   a. Have you presented your ideas in the most effective way?

   b. Are they ordered in concurrence with the organizational pattern that you are using?

4. Your concluding paragraph

   a. Have you signaled your concluding paragraph?

   b. Have you done one or more of the following?

      i. restated the thesis statement

      ii. summarized the body paragraphs

      iii. made a final comment

   c. Have you avoided adding any new ideas?

   d. Have you avoided adding any unnecessary details?

■ **PRACTICE 1: Evaluating an Introductory Paragraph**

Work with a classmate on evaluating the following introductory paragraph.
Check (✓) each statement that you agree with. Be prepared to explain your answers.

❑ The hook is effective.

❑ There is a smooth transition from the hook to the thesis statement.

❑ The thesis statement is the last statement in the introduction.

❑ The thesis statement has a clear topic and controlling idea.

Every day we are flooded with stimuli from electronic sources: MP3 players, cell phones, and computers. There are televisions, DVD players, radios, and video games keeping us occupied at home. At night, it is no wonder that when the stimuli is turned off as we get into bed, it is difficult for a lot of us to turn our brains off as well and get to sleep. In fact, many of us turn to sleeping aids to help us go to sleep. However, sleeping pills can cause considerable health problems. This is true for both the over-the-counter kind and prescriptions from doctors.

■ **PRACTICE 2: Evaluating a Concluding Paragraph**

Work with a classmate on evaluating the following concluding paragraph. Check (✓) each statement that you agree with. Be prepared to explain your answers.

❏ There is a signal indicating that this is the concluding paragraph.

❏ The thesis statement is restated.

❏ The body paragraphs are summarized.

❏ There is a final comment.

❏ There are no new ideas.

❏ There are no unnecessary details.

Not being able to get to sleep and stay asleep is a serious problem for many people, especially in our modern world of constant stimulation. Every day we are flooded with stimuli from electronic sources: MP3 players, cell phones, and computers. There are televisions, DVD players, radios, and video games keeping us occupied at home. It's not surprising that so many turn to sleeping pills, which may work. However, the danger is when they work too well, and users continue to use them. The drug companies recommend that you not use them for longer than thirty days, but I know people who have used them for years. The health problems that arise from prolonged use of over the counter and prescription medications for sleep are considerable. The irony is that one problem that often arises is insomnia. What is an insomniac to do? The best advice is to read a boring book and resolve to sleep better the following night.

> **What about you?**
> Share any concerns you have about the content of your paper with a classmate.

Checking the Content

Reread your essay carefully, concentrating on these areas:

1. The logic and legitimacy of your arguments
    a. Do your arguments make sense?
    b. Are enough of them supported by outside sources?
    c. Do any ideas need more outside support?
    d. Are the sources well chosen?
    e. Is the support truly relevant?

2. The unity of your paragraphs
    a. Are there any irrelevant ideas in your paragraphs?
    b. Does each sentence add to the explanation and support of the paragraph?
    c. Are there any redundancies? That is, are ideas repeated unnecessarily?

3. Your concrete support
    a. Have you included all the main ideas in your summaries?
    b. Have you maintained the meaning of your paraphrases?
    c. Have you used your own words and style in your summaries and paraphrases?
    d. Have you copied your quotes correctly?
    e. Have you cited each piece of concrete support?

■ PRACTICE 3: Evaluating a Body Paragraph

Below is a body paragraph from the paper "The Dangers of Sleeping Pills." With a classmate, evaluate it by discussing its arguments, paragraph unity, paragraph redundancy, and concrete support. Be prepared to make suggestions for improvement. The original passage for the concrete support is to the right of the paragraph.

American Society of Health-System Pharmacists

Zolpidem

(zole pi' dem)

Why is this medication prescribed?

Zolpidem is used to treat insomnia (difficulty falling asleep or staying asleep). Zolpidem belongs to a class of medications called sedative-hypnotics. It works by slowing activity in the brain to allow sleep.

How should this medicine be used?

Zolpidem comes as a tablet and an extended-release (long acting) tablet to take by mouth. It is usually taken as needed at bedtime. Zolpidem will work faster if it is not taken with a meal or immediately after a meal. Follow the directions on your prescription label carefully, and ask your doctor or pharmacist to explain any part you do not understand. Take zolpidem exactly as directed.

In addition to the side effects, there are the problems associated with becoming dependent on the pills. Prescription sleeping pills are meant to be taken for a short period of time—usually less than a month. You shouldn't take them for more than thirty days. If someone relies on a sleeping pill for longer than that, it may become more and more difficult to get to sleep without a pill. Once you become dependent on the pills, withdrawal from them can be very difficult. According to the American Society for Health-Systems Pharmacists, the ingredient zolpidem, common in some pills, may cause the taker to ". . . develop unpleasant feelings or . . . experience more severe withdrawal symptoms such as seizures, shakiness, stomach and muscle cramps, vomiting, sweating, and rarely, seizures" ("Zolpidem," 2008). As this list shows, the withdrawal can be difficult both physically and psychologically. It's clear that physical

(continued)

You will probably become very sleepy soon after you take zolpidem and will remain sleepy for some time after you take the medication. Plan to go to bed right after you take zolpidem, and to stay in bed for 7–8 hours. Do not take zolpidem if you will be unable to remain asleep for 7–8 hours after taking the medication. If you get up too soon after taking zolpidem, you may experience memory problems.

Swallow the extended release tablets whole; do not split, chew, or crush them.

Your sleep problems should improve within 7–10 days after you start taking zolpidem. Call your doctor if your sleep problems do not improve during this time or if they get worse at any time during your treatment.

Zolpidem should normally be taken for short periods of time. If you take zolpidem for 2 weeks or longer, zolpidem may not help you sleep as well as it did when you first began to take the medication. If you take zolpidem for a long time, you also may develop dependence ('addiction'; a need to continue taking the medication) on zolpidem. Talk to your doctor about the risks of taking zolpidem for 2 weeks or longer. Do not take a larger dose of zolpidem, take it more often, or take it for a longer time than prescribed by your doctor.

Do not stop taking zolpidem without talking to your doctor, especially if

withdrawal is worse than psychological withdrawal. It can be especially dangerous when the withdrawal symptom is insomnia. Users are trying to sleep, but the medication that they took to get them to sleep in the past is now causing them to not be able to sleep. It becomes a vicious cycle and hard to break out of. In addition, prescription sleeping pills are not cheap. If you don't have health insurance, they can be even more expensive.

(*continued*)

you have taken it for longer than 2 weeks. If you suddenly stop taking zolpidem, you may develop unpleasant feelings or you may experience more severe withdrawal symptoms such as seizures, shakiness, stomach and muscle cramps, vomiting, sweating, and rarely, seizures.

You may have more difficulty falling asleep or staying asleep on the first night after you stop taking zolpidem than you did before you started taking the medication. This is normal and usually gets better without treatment after one or two nights.

Ask your doctor or pharmacist for a copy of the manufacturer's information for the patient.

Checking Cohesiveness

In addition to having solid content and clear organization, your essay must function as one unit of writing; in other words, it must be **cohesive**. One idea should flow into another, and your readers should have no trouble following from one paragraph to another. Plenty of transitions help your reader move from one part of your essay to another.

In Chapter 1, you combined sentences with **transition words**, such as *however* and *therefore*, and **transition phrases**, such as *as a result* and *in addition*. To review these, see Appendix 2 on pages 164–165.

You also learned about **transition sentences**, called bridges, in Chapter 1. These complete sentences come at the end of a body paragraph to connect it to the following paragraph, or at the beginning of a paragraph (often before the topic sentence) as a connection from the previous paragraph.

In addition to using these for cohesion, you can use a **transition paragraph** to connect one section of your paper to another section. In the diagram on page 143, the transition paragraph connects the section that discusses over-the-counter sleeping pills to the section that discusses prescription medications.

Introductory paragraph

Thesis: However, sleeping pills, both the over-the-counter kind and prescriptions, can cause considerable health problems.

Section 1: Over-the-Counter Sleeping Pills

Paragraph 1

Antihistamines

Paragraph 2

Herbal medications

Transition paragraph

While the over-the-counter sleep medications have side effects, the truly dangerous effects come with the prescription medications for zolpidem and eszopiclone. These are examples of a type of drug called hypnotics. Hypnotics make you sleep, but also they can make you become semi-conscious. They claim to offer a good night's sleep, and they do. However, they also offer much more.

Section 2: Prescription Sleeping Pills

Paragraph 1

Side effects

Paragraph 2

Dependency and withdrawal

Paragraph 3

Dangerous behaviors

Concluding paragraph

■ PRACTICE 4: Using Transition Paragraphs

Look at the following outlines and discuss with a classmate whether a transition paragraph would be useful in the paper. If so, discuss where it should go.

Outline 1

    I. *Thesis statement:* The causes of chronic insomnia invariably lead to serious effects.

   II. Too much outside stimulation

  III. Too many internal worries

  IV. Trouble focusing the next day

   V. Long-term health issues

  VI. Conclusion

Outline 2

    I. *Thesis statement:* Although they have similarities, zolpidem and eszopiclone have more differences.

   II. Both are effective.

  III. Both can cause memory loss.

  IV. Zolpidem is more addictive than eszopiclone.

   V. Zolpidem's side effects are more severe.

  VI. Eszopiclone is more user friendly than zolpidem in terms of taste, quality of sleep, and next-day effects.

 VII. Conclusion

Outline 3

<table>
<tr><td>

What about you?

Would your paper be better with a transition paragraph? Discuss it with a classmate.

</td><td>

    I. *Thesis statement:* As we age, our sleep requirements change.

   II. Babies

  III. Children

  IV. Teens

   V. Adults

  VI. Elderly

 VII. Conclusion

</td></tr>
</table>

Editing

When you are finished revising your paper, you can edit it by checking for grammar, punctuation, and spelling mistakes. You should also check the documentation to be sure that your in-text citations and References list have the appropriate format.

■ **PRACTICE 4: Editing for Mistakes with Grammar and Punctuation**

Work with a classmate to find and correct the six mistakes in grammar and punctuation in the body paragraph below.

> The other type of over-the-counter sleep aid is herbal. These remedies is often present in nighttime teas, such as chamomile, valerian root, and passion flower. These tea are generally considered safe and nontoxic. Although there are cautions about using some with alcohol or while pregnant. The other natural remedy is the hormone melatonin, this helps regulate the clock in our bodies by being sensitive to light and darkness. Melatonin levels reduce in the light and increase in the dark so if you take it, simulates darkness and cues your body to sleep. Taking melatonin can also result in daytime sleepiness and headaches (Berge, 2007). Thus, the very reason for taking melatonin—to get a good night's sleep so that the next day you can do what you need to do—can be negated by taking it.

■ **PRACTICE 5: Editing for Mistakes with Citations**

Work with a classmate to find and correct the three mistakes with citations in the body paragraph below. Refer to Chapter 5, pages 80–81, for help if necessary.

> The final negative effect of hypnotic sleeping pills is that they may cause bizarre behavior while sleeping. For example, several people have reported binge eating while sleeping. This means that these people have woken up and found evidence of someone having eaten a lot during the night in their bedroom and in their kitchen. (Saul 2007). There are at least 30 documented cases of "sleep eating." Perhaps the most dangerous behavior is driving while sleeping. An article in the New York Times by Stephanie Saul reports "Sleep-drivers reported frightening episodes in which they recalled going to bed, but woke up to find they had been arrested roadside in their underwear or nightclothes." These odd side effects have caused the FDA to order the makers of these drugs to put strong labels on the bottles that warn the users of the dangers of the potential side effects.

■ *PRACTICE 6*: **Editing a References List**

Work with a classmate to find and correct the six mistakes in the References list below. Refer to Chapter 5, pages 77–79, for help if necessary.

References

Zolpidem. (2007, August 1). American Society of Health-System Pharmacists. Retrieved April 4, 2008 from http://www.ncbli.nlm.nih .gov/books/'bv.fcgi?log$=drug_bottom_one&rid=medmaster .chaptera693025.

Berge, K. (October 18, 2007). Melatonin side effects: What are the risks? November 30, 2007 from http://www.mayoclinic.com/health/ melatonin-side-effects/AN01717MayoClinic.com.

Zolpidem. (2007 August). Consumer Reports Health. Retrieved December 31, 2007 from http://www.consumerreports.org/health/drug-reports/ zolpidem.htm.

Saul, Stephanie. (2007, March 15). U.S. calls for Strong Warnings on Sleep Aids' Strange Effects. *New York Times* p. A1.

Guidelines for Research Paper Format

1. In the heading section of each page, put the title of your paper and the page number. If your title is longer than fifty letters, abbreviate it.

The Dangers of Sleeping Pills 1

2. Center the title of your paper and your name in the upper half of the page. Center the name of the class, the name of the professor, and the date at the bottom of the page.

The Dangers of Sleeping Pills 1

The Dangers of Sleeping Pills

Leandro Sanchez

English 101

Professor Marsh

December 12, 2008

3. On the first page of your research paper, center the title of your paper, and begin your introductory paragraph on the (double-spaced) line.

> The Dangers of Sleeping Pills 2
>
>
> The Dangers of Sleeping Pills
>
> Every day we are flooded with stimuli from electronic
>
> sources: MP3 players, cell phones, and computers. There are
>
> televisions, DVD players radios and video games keeping us
>
> occupied at home. At

4. Double space. Do not leave an extra space between paragraphs.

5. Your References list should be on a separate page.

Sample Short Research Paper

Review the sample research paper with the highlighted notes.

The Dangers of Sleeping Pills 1
heading includes title of paper and page number

The Dangers of Sleeping Pills
centered title

Leandro Sanchez
centered author's name

English 101
name of class centered

Professor Marsh
name of professor

December 12, 2008
date

The Dangers of Sleeping Pills
centered title on first page

Every day we are flooded with stimuli from electronic sources: MP3 players, cell phones, and computers. There are televisions, DVD players, radios, and video games keeping us occupied at home. At night, it is no wonder that when the stimuli are turned off as we get into bed, it is difficult to turn our brains off as well and get to sleep. In fact, many of us turn to sleeping aids to help us go to sleep. For the most part, these work well, and we soon drift off to sleep. However, sleeping pills, both the over-the-counter kind and prescriptions, can cause considerable health problems.

no extra space between paragraphs

There are basically two types of sleeping aids that you can get without a prescription, called "over-the-counter." The first contains antihistamines called diphenhydramine hydrochloride or doxylamine succinate. Antihistamines are used when you have a cold to clear up your runny nose. You also take antihistamines when you have allergies. The biggest danger of using antihistamines is that they make you drowsy. In fact, the labels on these medications indicate that you shouldn't take them before driving. In fact the drowsiness from antihistamines can last longer than a typical 8-hour night's sleep, so using these may help you sleep, but they are not good for the next day's work.

The other type of over-the-counter sleep aid is herbal. These remedies are often present in nighttime teas, such as

chamomile, valerian root, and passion flower. These teas are generally considered safe and nontoxic although there are cautions about using some with alcohol or while pregnant. The other natural remedy is the hormone melatonin, which helps regulate the clock in our bodies by being sensitive to light and darkness. Melatonin levels decrease in the light and increase in the dark, so if you take it, it simulates darkness and cues your body to sleep. However, taking melatonin can also result in daytime sleepiness and headaches (Berge, 2007). *in-text citation for summary*
Thus, the very reason for taking melatonin—to get a good night's sleep so that the next day you can do what you need to do—can be negated by taking it.

While the over-the-counter sleep medications have side effects, the truly dangerous effects come with the prescription medications. These medications are called tranquilizers and sedatives because they make the users quiet by slowing down their central nervous systems. They work a lot like alcohol and can make the user depressed as well as sleepy. In the past fifteen years, new types of prescription sleeping pills have come onto the market. These medications, which contain such ingredients as zolpidem and eszopiclone, are supposed to be better than the old tranquilizers, but they, too, have serious health consequences. They are examples of a type of drug called hypnotics. Hypnotics make you sleep, but also they can make you semi-conscious. They claim to offer a good night's sleep, and they do. However, they also offer much more.

According to the *Consumer Reports* webpage, there are
italicize names of magazines
twenty-two side effects that could occur when you take zolpidem. These range from drowsiness to neck pain. In addition, there are thirteen more side effects that you should call a doctor about should they occur. These include difficulty breathing, chest pain, and blurred vision ("Zolpidem," 2007, August). That's a total of thirty-five ways
citation for summary uses brief title in quotation marks if no author
that this sleeping pill could possibly hurt the user's body. Furthermore, these possible damages could increase with prolonged use of the drug. It's clear that using a sleeping pill with zolpidem is dangerous for your health.

In addition to the side effects, there are the problems associated with becoming dependent on the pills. Prescription sleeping pills are meant to be taken for a short period of time—usually less than a month. If someone relies on a sleeping pill longer than that, it may become more and more difficult to get to sleep without a pill. Once you become dependent on the pills, withdrawal from them can be very difficult. According to the American Society for Health-Systems Pharmacists, the ingredient zolpidem, common in some pills, may cause the taker to ". . . develop unpleasant feelings
ellipses indicate a deletion from the original
or . . . experience more severe withdrawal symptoms such as seizures, shakiness, stomach and muscle cramps, vomiting, sweating, and rarely, seizures" ("Zolpidem," 2007, August 1).
citation for quotation with no author

As this list shows, the withdrawal can be difficult both psychologically and physically. It can be especially dangerous when the withdrawal symptom is insomnia. Users are trying to sleep, but the medication that they took to get them to sleep in the past is now causing them to not be able to sleep. It becomes a vicious cycle and hard to break.

The final negative effect of hypnotic sleeping pills is that they may cause bizarre behavior while sleeping. For example, several people have reported binge eating while sleeping. This means that these people have woken up and found evidence of someone having eaten a lot during the night in their bedroom and in their kitchen (Saul, 2007). There are at least 30

citation for paraphrase

documented cases of "sleep eating." Perhaps the most dangerous behavior is driving while sleeping. An article in *The New York Times* by Stephanie Saul reports, "Sleep-drivers reported frightening episodes in which they recalled going to bed, but woke up to find they had been arrested roadside in their underwear or nightclothes" (2007, p. A1). These odd side

use page number in citation after a quote

effects have caused the FDA to order the makers of these drugs to put strong labels on the bottles that warn the users of the dangers of the potential side effects.

In conclusion, not being able to get to sleep and stay asleep is a serious problem for many people, especially in our modern world of constant stimulation. It's not surprising that so many turn to sleeping pills, which may work. However, the danger is when they work too well and users continue

to use them. The health problems that arise from prolonged

use of OTC and prescription medications for sleep are

considerable. The irony is that one problem that often arises

is insomnia. What is an insomniac to do? The best advice

is to read a boring book and resolve to sleep better the

following night.

References list on separate page

references listed in alphabetical order by author's last name or by title

References

"References" centered

Berge, K. (2007, October 18). Melatonin side effects: What

are the risks? Retrieved November 30, 2007 from

divide urls only before and after slashes

http://www.mayoclinic.com/health/melatonin-side-effects/

AN01717MayoClinic.com.

Saul, S. (2007, March 15). U.S. calls for strong warnings on

sleep aids' strange effects [Electronic version].

The New York Times, p. A1.

Zolpidem. (2007, August 1). American Society of Health-

title of unauthored article

System Pharmacists. Retrieved April 4, 2008 from

first line only of each entry indented

http://www.ncbli.nlm.nih.gov/books/'bv.fcgi?log$=drug_

bottom_one&rid=medmaster.chaptera693025.

Zolpidem. (2007, August). Consumer Reports Health. Retrieved

December 31, 2007 from http://www.consumerreports.

org/health/drug-reports/zolpidem.htm.

Avoiding Unclear Comparisons

Comparing two items is often a good way to analyze them. For the comparisons to be effective, however, they must be clear.

1. Add a verb or an auxiliary verb if there is doubt about the function of the noun following the comparison. For example:

   ➤ When we were in France, we didn't go as far as Nancy.

   In this example, it's unclear whether Nancy is referring to the name of a city or the name of a person. If you are talking about the French city called Nancy, the sentence is fine. However, if you are talking about a person, then you need to add a verb or auxiliary verb after the subject:

   ➤ When we were in France, we didn't go as far as Nancy **went**.

   ➤ When we were in France, we didn't go as far as Nancy **did**.

2. Add possessives to be sure that the two items that you are comparing can be compared. For example:

   ✗ My research paper wasn't as long as Lin.

   In this example, the sentence sounds as if it is comparing the length of a research paper to the length of a person. Clearly, this is not the intent of the writer. To be clear that you are comparing the length of one paper to the length of another, you need to add a possessive pronoun.

   ➤ My research paper wasn't as long as Lin's research paper.

   ➤ My research paper wasn't as long as Lin's.

3. Use *the one* or *those* as pronouns to make two comparisons clear. For example:

   ✗ The library in my hometown doesn't have as many books as Paolo.

   ✗ The libraries in my hometown don't have as many books as Paolo.

   It's unlikely that the writer intends to compare a library to a man. It's more likely that the comparison is between two libraries in two different hometowns. To make it clear, you can say:

   ➤ The library in my hometown doesn't have as many books as **the one** in Paolo's hometown.

   ➤ The libraries in my hometown don't have as many books as **those** in Paolo's hometown.

■ **PRACTICE 7: Evaluating Comparisons**

Read each sentence below and determine whether the comparison is clear. If it is not, be prepared to explain why and to suggest a sentence that makes the comparison clearer. Work with a classmate.

1. Isabel likes her cat more than her husband.

2. My English literature class was smaller than Rebecca.

3. The number of citations in Carla's paper was greater than Donna's.

4. The radio in the car doesn't work as well as the house.

5. You spent as much time in the library as I.

6. The professors in the English Department give much more homework than in the Psychology Department.

7. I would rather spend time with books than Ching and his wife.

8. The meeting I went to in San Francisco was more useful than the one in Toronto.

III LANGUAGE FOCUS

Commonly Confused Words: Prepositions and Pronouns

Both native and non-native speakers confuse the pairs of words below. Study the definitions and sample sentences to understand the difference between the two words in each pair.

1. **among** *prep.* affecting many people in a particular group

   between *prep.* used to show the relationship between two situations, things, or people

   ➤ Although we were **among** many people, I felt a special connection **between** you and me.

2. **beside** *prep.* next to or very close to something or someone

   besides *conj.* in addition (to)

   ➤ **Besides** wanting to ride to the restaurant with me, Margaret insisted that I sit **beside** her at dining table.

3. **it's** *subject pron. and v.* the short form of "it is"

   its *possessive pron.* belonging to or relating to a thing, situation, person, or idea that is known

   ➤ **It's** very dark outside, but we can still see the black cat because **its** eyes are reflecting the moonlight.

4. **there** *pron.* used to say that something exists; in or to a particular place that is not near where you are

   their *possessive pron.* belonging to or relating to people, animals, or things that are known

   they're *subject pron. and v.* the short form of "they are"

   ➤ **They're** going to meet us **there** with **their** new dog.

5. **we're** *subject pron. and v.* the short form for "we are"

   were *v.* third person plural past tense of "be"

   ➤ **We're** going on vacation to the same place you **were** last year.

6. **your** *possessive pron.* belonging to or relating to the person or people someone is speaking to

   you're *subject pron. and v.* the short form for "you are"

   ➤ **You're** going to drive **your** own car, right?

■ *PRACTICE 8:* **Choosing the Correct Word**

Choose the correct word to go in each blank by circling it. Then compare your answers with a classmate.

Sleeping Arrangements

Said the tour leader to the tired travelers, "Please listen while I tell you

where you will sleep tonight. _____ all going to have to share a
(1. You're / Your)

room, and some people _____ you have to share with two other
(2. among / between)

people. _____ in a small hotel, and _____ aren't
(3. We're / Were)   (4. there / their / they're)

enough rooms for everyone. _____, _____ more fun
(5. Beside / Besides)   (6. it's / its)

to share a room, don't you think? José and Chang? _____
(7. Your / You're)

room is on the fourth floor. _____ sharing with Todd. Maria and
(8. Your / You're)

Susanna? Where are those two? Will someone tell them that _____
(9. there / their / they're)

room is on the third floor? On the second floor, there is one single room

_____ the elevator. I'll take that one because _____
(10. beside / besides)   (11. it's / its)

bed is quite small. Does everyone know where they're going? Good. Good

night, everyone. I'll see you in the morning."

Your Turn

At last, you are ready to revise and edit the paper you have been working on. Use the lists of questions on pages 137–138 to focus your attention. Then, submit your paper in good research paper format. Your instructor may ask you to submit copies of your original sources and your first draft.

Peer Help Worksheet

Read a classmate's research paper while he or she reads yours. Then discuss the answers to these questions.

CONTENT

1 What did you like most about your classmate's paper? _____

_____

_____

_____

2 What did you learn that most surprised or interested you? _____

_____

_____

_____

3 Were the arguments in the paper well articulated? . . . . ❑

4 Was the paper convincing? . . . . ❑

ORGANIZATION

1 Was the paper well organized? . . . . ❑

2 Was it easy to follow? . . . . ❑

LANGUAGE

1 Was there any part of the essay you could not
understand because of grammar? . . . . ❑

2 Was the paper formatted correctly? . . . . ❑

Discuss any possible mistakes with the writer.

Writing to Communicate . . . More

As a journal entry or an in-class essay, choose one of the topics below to write about.

1. Reflect on the research process that you have just completed.
   a. Was it a positive experience?
   b. What did you learn?
   c. What did you do well?
   d. What will you do differently the next time you have to write a research paper?
2. Reflect on your understanding of academic writing.
   a. What have you learned?
   b. How has your writing improved?
   c. What area(s) needs more improvement?
   d. What more about academic writing would you like to learn?
3. Reflect on your future goals in writing.
   a. How has the experience of writing a research paper prepared you for your future academic life?
   b. Do you enjoy writing? Do you think it will be part of your future after you finish studying?

I REVIEWING IDEAS/ERROR ANALYSIS

With a classmate, evaluate the following short research paper. Answer the questions in the margins. If any boxes are not checked, discuss with your classmate how the writer could correct the paper.

1. Is the title page correctly formatted? ❏

2. Is the title appropriate for the paper? ❏

3. Is the capitalization correct? ❏

The Effects of Insomnia 1

The effects of Insomnia

Georgia Hwang

English 101

Edwin R. Marsh

12 December 2008

The Effects of Insomnia

Most people know that you are supposed to get eight hours of sleep each night, but less than half of people in the United States get that much. The other half suffer from insomnia. The causes of insomnia are fairly well known, but its effects are not.

The first cause is too much outside stimulation. People are too distracted, and they can stay that way long after dark. Patricia Corrigan in the *St. Louis Dispatch* quotes Dr. Stephanie Zoberi, who points out, "'Now when the sun goes down, instead of ending the day as our ancestors did, we go to the movies, do household chores, watch TV or head for the mall'." (2003) People may stay up playing video games until they can't keep their eyes open any longer. Then, they wonder why they have trouble getting up in the morning.

In addition to outside distractions, many people have trouble sleeping due to internal distractions. They replay the day and think about what they could have done or might have said in a certain situation. They may also worry about what is going to happen the next day. Will their presentation go well? Will they be able to find the restaurant? Will their children get sick? They go over and over scenarios about what they will do if something happens. Then, all of a sudden, morning happens, and they have to get up. "Some people," says Corrigan, "of course, suffer from sleep disorders. And studies show most people deal with sleep disorders on their own,

4. Does the introductory paragraph have a clear thesis statement? ❏

5. Does the quotation in the first body paragraph support the writer's argument? ❏

6. Is the quotation properly cited? ❏

7. Are all of the arguments relevant to the topic sentence? ❏

8. Does the concrete support on this page support the writer's argument? ❏

9. Is the concrete support properly cited? ❏

10. Circle all the transitions used on this page.

11. Find and correct the three language mistakes on this page.

12. Do the body paragraphs have topic sentences? ❏

13. Do the body paragraphs have concluding sentences? ❏

14. There are three missing commas on this page. Add them.

15. Underline the bridge on this page.

16. Does the concrete support on this page support the writer's argument? ❏

17. Is the concrete support properly cited? ❏

perhaps choosing an over-the-counter medication at the pharmacy or grocery" (Corrigan, 2003, p. NA).

Whether you can't sleep because of outside distractions or inside worries, the effects on your life and on your health can be detrimental.

The most immediate effect occurs the day after have trouble sleeping. Not sleeping enough makes it difficult to concentrate on what you are supposed to be doing. It might take you twice as long to complete a task. Then, you get irritating because of your inefficiency. You may snap at your coworkers or throw something. Moreover, you will also probably feel drowsy next day. You might even fall asleep at the office. While this may get you fired, it won't kill you. However if your job is a truck driver and you fall asleep, you could end up killing yourself and others. This danger is serious but it isn't the only serious danger.

The real danger of not getting enough sleep lies in its long term effects on your health. First of all, sleep is very important to your physical health. While sleeping, you are allowing your body enough time to heal itself from the day's exertions. Experts say not getting enough sleep for a long period can lead to the lowering of your immune system heart problems and diabetes. (Corrigan, 2003). Second, you may experience mental problems, such as having trouble remembering things and becoming depressed. We need to sleep to give our minds a chance to rest and to "get rid of nonsense" (Corrigan).

The Effects of Insomnia 4

All in all, it's clear that getting enough sleep is important to our physical and mental health. If you are not getting at least eight hours of sleep each night, you should change your ways! Then, your life will be better.

18. Is the concluding paragraph well written? ❏

19. Is the References page properly formatted? ❏

20. Is the entry properly formatted? ❏

The Effects of Insomnia 5

References

Patricia Corrigan. (2003, September 5). Experts say that Sleep is vital to our Well-Being. *St. Louis Dispatch.*

II LANGUAGE REVIEW

Circle the correct word to go in each blank. Then compare your answers with a classmate.

Time and the Research Paper

It is imperative that students writing a research paper _____
(1. devote / devotes)
many hours to _____ completion. At first, students _____
(2. it's / its)   (3. maybe / may be)
tempted to put off beginning _____ research since they have
(4. there / their / they're)
probably been given some time to do it. This is _____ a good idea.
(5. hard / hardly)
The due date for the paper will come sooner _____ they expect.
(6. than / then)
_____, they may need to change their topic once or twice, and
(7. Beside / Besides)
_____ better to have more time than not enough. Students must be
(8. it's / its)
_____ with _____ time, so they don't have trouble finishing
(9. economic / economical) (10. there / their / they're)
by the due date. Most professors recommend that at least two hours each day
_____ spent on doing research and on writing. Of course, this
(11. are / be / is)
number will no doubt increase as the due date gets closer. In short, students
must spend a lot of time writing _____ research papers.
(12. there / their / they're)

For short papers (fewer than five typed pages), it is not necessary to have a cover page. Follow the format below or ask your instructor for any special requirements.

1

page number in the upper right-hand corner

Min Hee Kim *(First name Last name)*
English 101 *(Name of class)*
February 6, 2008 *(Month day, year)*

entire paper after the heading is double spaced

The Qualities of Friendship
centered title, plain text

→ There is an old adage in English that says that, while we may
each paragraph indented 5 spaces (1 tab)
be stuck with our relatives, we get to choose our friends. This

can be a joy, but it also carries the responsibility of choosing our
no space between a word and a comma
friends wisely. To me, a person must have certain qualities in or-

der for us to become friends. Among many, I can identify three

that are essential: a sense of humor, steadfastness, and caring.
no extra space between paragraphs
→ The first important quality that I value in a friend is a sense of

humor. Life should be enjoyed, and there is no better way to enjoy

it than with a good laugh. Life can also be full of difficulties, and
no space between a word and a period
sometimes the only way to get through them is to laugh. In both

good and bad times, laughing is good for the body and good for

the soul. My best friend, Pam, is an example of someone I can

laugh with in any situation. She and I grew up together because

our mothers were best friends. Because of this, we have very sim-

ilar senses of humor. Although we live close together now, we lived

in different states or different countries for many years after we

grew up. The distance didn't change us. In fact, we spent hours

on the phone laughing so hard that we had tears in our eyes. I

suspect that Pam and I will be laughing together well into our old

age. I believe that our friendship has lasted so many years and

will last many more because we are able to laugh together.

COMMON CONNECTORS

	Chronology		Cause	Result	Unexpected Result	Contrast	Direct Contrast
TRANSITIONS	first at first second third next after that	at this point later on then at last finally		as a consequence as a result consequently therefore	however nevertheless nonetheless	however in contrast	however on the other hand
CONJUNCTIONS — SUBORDINATING	after as before since	until when while	as because since		although even though		whereas while
CONJUNCTIONS — COORDINATING	and		for	so	but yet	but yet	but yet
PREPOSITIONS	after before since	until prior to	because of due to		despite in spite of	different from in contrast to	unlike

	Similarity	Addition	Example	Explanation	Emphasis	Condition	Conclusion
TRANSITIONS	likewise similarly	in addition moreover furthermore	for example for instance	that is in other words	indeed in fact	otherwise in that case	in short in conclusion in summary to sum up all in all
CONJUNCTIONS — SUBORDINATING							
CONJUNCTIONS — COORDINATING	both . . . and neither . . . nor not only . . . but also	and					
PREPOSITIONS	like similar to	in addition to					

Below is a worksheet that will take you through the steps of the writing process.

Step 1: Understanding the Assignment

Before you begin, be sure that you understand the details of the assignment. Fill in these boxes with the pertinent information. Ask your instructor about any information that you do not know.

Topic	Purpose	Source of Information	Length	Due Date	Format

Step 2: Brainstorming Ideas

Remember that the most important task of brainstorming is to get as many ideas about your topic as possible. Here is the start of a circle diagram. Put your narrowed topic in the circle, and write ideas on the lines. Add lines coming from the lines to elaborate on one topic.

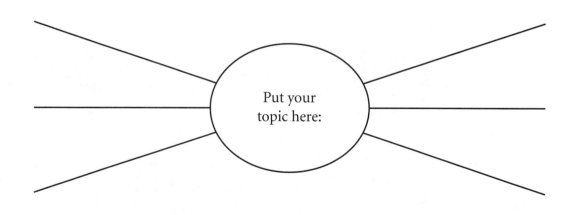

Put your
topic here:

Step 3: Organizing Your Ideas

1. *Decide what you want to say about your topic. Form this into a controlling idea and then write your working thesis statement.*

2. *Are there any ideas from Step 2 that do not relate to your thesis statement? If so, cross them out.*

3. *Complete this outline with the relevant ideas from Step 2 and any additional ideas that come to you. You may need to increase or decrease the number of body paragraphs and the number of major supporting sentences and minor supporting sentences within each body paragraph. At this point, you do not have to write complete sentences. Writing notes is enough.*

I. Introductory paragraph

   a. Hook _____

   b. Connection _____

   c. Thesis statement _____

   _____

II. Body paragraph 1

   a. Topic sentence _____

     i. Major supporting sentence _____

     _____

      1. Minor supporting sentence _____

      _____

      2. Minor supporting sentence _____

      _____

     ii. Major supporting sentence _____

     _____

      1. Minor supporting sentence _____

      _____

      2. Minor supporting sentence _____

      _____

     iii. Major supporting sentence _____

     _____

      1. Minor supporting sentence _____

      _____

      2. Minor supporting sentence _____

      _____

   b. Concluding sentence or bridge (optional) _____

   _____

III. Body paragraph 2

    a. Topic sentence or bridge (optional) _____

    _____

       i. Major supporting sentence _____

       _____

         1. Minor supporting sentence _____

         _____

         2. Minor supporting sentence _____

         _____

       ii. Major supporting sentence _____

       _____

         1. Minor supporting sentence _____

         _____

         2. Minor supporting sentence _____

         _____

       iii. Major supporting sentence _____

       _____

         1. Minor supporting sentence _____

         _____

         2. Minor supporting sentence _____

         _____

    b. Concluding sentence or bridge (optional) _____

    _____

IV. Body paragraph 3

    a. Topic sentence or bridge (optional) _____

    _____

       i. Major supporting sentence _____

       _____

         1. Minor supporting sentence _____

         _____

         2. Minor supporting sentence _____

         _____

       ii. Major supporting sentence _____

       _____

    1. Minor supporting sentence _____

    _____

    2. Minor supporting sentence _____

    _____

iii. Major supporting sentence _____

    _____

    1. Minor supporting sentence _____

    _____

    2. Minor supporting sentence _____

    _____

b. Concluding sentence (optional) _____

    _____

V. Concluding paragraph

    a. restatement of thesis statement and/or _____

    _____

    b. summary of points in body paragraph and/or _____

    _____

    c. final comment _____

    _____

Step 4: Writing the First Draft

Write the first draft from your outline. Many writers find it useful to write the thesis statement first, add the body paragraphs, and then write the introductory and concluding paragraphs. Some writers type their essays and save them so that further drafts are easier to change. Other writers prefer to write their first draft by hand. You need to discover which method works best for you. As you write, other relevant ideas may occur to you. Add them as appropriate.

Put your paper aside for at least an hour before moving on to Step 5.

Step 5: Rewriting the First Draft

*To get another perspective on your essay, you may want to complete this step with a classmate. You can exchange papers and use the General Peer Help Worksheet in Appendix 4 or the questions below to evaluate each other's essays. Rewriting consists of two parts: **revising** and **editing**.*

1. To *revise* your paper, answer these questions:

Content:
    a. Is there a logical connection from the hook to the thesis statement in your introductory paragraph?

    b. Are all the ideas in your body paragraphs relevant?

    c. Is there adequate support for your thesis statement?

Organization:
    a. Is your thesis statement at the end of your introductory paragraph?

    b. Do you need topic sentences in your body paragraphs?

    c. Are there adequate transitions?

    d. Would a bridge from one paragraph to another make your essay easier to understand?

    e. Is your concluding paragraph appropriate?

Vocabulary:
    a. Are your words too informal for academic writing?

    b. Can you use a more descriptive word or a more accurate word?

2. To *edit* your paper, check for grammar and punctuation mistakes.

> Before writing your final draft, you may find it helpful to repeat Steps 4 and 5.

Step 6: Writing the Final Draft

Write your final draft, correcting the mistakes you found in Step 5.

The Peer Help Worksheets that appear throughout this book are designed to help you look at your writing with a critical eye. Many of the worksheets in the book focus on one particular topic, but the worksheet below is more general and can be used to help you evaluate an academic essay with or without outside concrete support. Once you have read your classmate's paper and gone through the worksheet, share your thoughts with your classmate.

CONTENT

1 What did you particularly like about this essay? _____
_____

2 What is the rhetorical pattern used in this essay? _____

3 Is the support in each body paragraph relevant
to the paragraph and to the thesis statement? . . . . ❑

4 Is there enough support for the arguments in the paper? . . . . . . ❑

ORGANIZATION

1 Does the introductory paragraph have a hook and
a clear connection to the thesis statement? . . . . ❑

2 In the thesis statement, circle the topic, underline the controlling
idea, and put a box around the predictor (if any).

3 Do the body paragraphs have good coherence?
That is, are they presented in a logical way? . . . . ❑

4 What elements does the concluding paragraph
in this essay have? _____

MECHANICS

1 Are capital letters, periods, commas, semicolons,
and quotation marks used appropriately? . . . . ❑

2 Did the writer avoid fragments, comma splices,
and run-on sentences? . . . . ❑

3 Does the essay have correct format, including
citations and a References list, if necessary? . . . . ❑

EVALUATION RUBRICS

There are many things to consider when evaluating academic writing. While different teachers and schools will use their own evaluation tools, most will include categories similar to those outlined in the form below.

SCORING	ASPECTS OF GOOD WRITING
Content/Ideas	
Very good: 25–23 Good: 22–20 Average: 19–17 Needs work: 16–0 SCORE:	• adheres to assignment parameters • has excellent and relevant concrete support (if any) • has well written summaries and paraphrases (if any) • has unity
Organization	
Very good: 25–23 Good: 22–20 Average: 19–17 Needs work: 16–0 SCORE:	• has introductory paragraph with clear thesis statement • has body paragraphs with good organization • has concluding paragraph • has coherence and cohesion
Grammar/Structure	
Very good: 25–23 Good: 22–20 Average: 19–17 Needs work: 16–0 SCORE:	• demonstrates control of basic grammar (e.g., tenses, verb forms, noun forms, preposition, articles) • shows sophistication of sentence structure with complex and compound sentences
Word Choice/Word Form	
Very good: 15–14 Good: 13–12 Average: 11–10 Needs work: 9–0 SCORE:	• demonstrates sophisticated choice of vocabulary items • has correct idiomatic use of vocabulary • has correct word forms
Mechanics	
Very good: 10 Good: 9–8 Average: 7–6 Needs work: 5–0 SCORE:	• has good essay format (including title page, if necessary) • demonstrates good control over use of capital letters, periods, commas, semicolons, and quotation marks • doesn't have fragments, comma splices, or run-on sentences • has correctly used in-text citations (if necessary) • has a References list with correctly written entries (if necessary)
Comments	
TOTAL SCORE:	

MLA DOCUMENTATION

The documentation style used in this text has been from the American Psychological Association (APA). It is the style most commonly used in social and behavioral sciences. This appendix presents an alternate documentation style from the Modern Languages Association (MLA). MLA is most commonly used in the humanities.

I. Making a Works Cited List

*A **Works Cited** list is like a References list in that it is a formal list of the sources that you cited in your paper. It is on a separate page after the last page of your paper. The entries are placed in alphabetical order according to the first word in the entries. (Use the second word if the first word is a, an, or the.) Look at the following basic entry formats.*

Abbreviations used in the explanations below

- ALN   author's last name
- AFN   author's first name
- ELN   editor's last name
- EFN   editor's first name
- n.d.   no date
- url   universal resource locator (the address of a Web site)

Definitions used in the explanations below

- Volume   A grouping of individual magazines or journals
- Issue   An individual magazine or journal
- Posting Date   The date that something is added to a Web site

Basic entry format for a book

1. One author

ALN, AFN. <u>Book Title</u>. Place of Publication: Publisher, Year.

Cooper, Anderson. <u>Dispatches from the Edge</u>. New York: HarperCollins Publishers, 2006.

2. Two or three authors

List the first author's last name and first name. List the second and third author's first name and last name.

ALN, AFN, and AFN ALN. <u>Book Title</u>. Place of Publication: Publisher, Year.

Lindenmayer, Clem, and Nick Tapp. <u>Trekking in the Patagonian Andes</u>. Melbourne: Lonely Planet Publications, 2007.

3. More than three authors

List the first author's last name and first name followed by et al. Everything else remains the same.
ALN, AFN, et al.

4. Editor

ELN, EFN, ed. <u>Book Title</u>.
  Place of Publication:
  Publisher, Year.

McCauley, Lucy, ed. <u>The Best Women's Travel Writing</u>. Berkeley: Publishers Group West, 2005.

5. Two or more editors

Use the same rules for editors that were described above for authors.

Basic entry format for a journal article

1. Pagination within one issue

ALN, AFN. "Name of Article."
  <u>Name of Publication</u> Volume
  Number. Issue Number
  (Year): page(s).

Lukinbeal, C. "Cinematic Landscapes." <u>Journal of Cultural Geography</u> 23.1 (2005):3.

2. Pagination continuous throughout volume

ALN, AFN. "Name of Article."
  <u>Name of Publication</u> Volume
  Number (Year): page(s).

Winter, Brian. "How Slim Got Huge." <u>Foreign Policy</u> 163 (2006):34–42.

Basic entry format for a magazine article

Note: Abbreviate the name of months except for May, June, and July.

1. One author

ALN, AFN. "Title of Article."
  <u>Name of Magazine</u> Day Month
  Year: page(s).

Heron, Mick. "A Terrible Case of Itchy Feet." <u>Geographical</u> 1 Feb. 2007: 90.

2. No author

"Title of Article."
  <u>Name of Magazine</u> Day Month
  Year: page(s).

"The Mother of All Travelogues." <u>Photo District News</u> 2 Dec. 2005: 104.

Basic entry format for a newspaper article

1. One author

ALN, AFN. "Title of Article."
  <u>Name of Newspaper</u> Day
  Month Year: page(s).

Olster, Alex. "Unwelcome Drama in Fall Tourism." <u>Boston Globe</u> 14 Oct. 2007: 4.

2. No author

"Title of Article."
　　Name of Newspaper Day
　　Month Year: page(s).

"Grounded Expectations." <u>Bangor Daily News</u> 7 Jan. 2008: 6.

Basic entry format for a Web site

Note: Divide urls before or after a slash (if possible).

1. General Web page

"Title of Page." <u>Name of Web Site</u>.
　　Posting Date. Access Date <url>.

"California History." <u>California: Find Yourself Here</u>. 2008. 26 Feb. 2008 <*http://www.visitcalifornia.com/AM/Template.cfm?Section=History&Template=/TaggedPage/TaggedPageDisplay.cfm&TPLID=5&ContentID=2277&cttcTemplate=lifestyle2/History/>*.

2. Online periodicals

ALN, AFN. "Title of Article."
　　<u>Title of Online Publication</u>
　　Posting Date. Access Date <url>.

Keillor, Garrison. "Just Follow the Map." <u>Salon.com</u>. 2 Jan. 2008. 11 Jan. 2008 <*http://www.salon.com/opinion/keillor/2008/01/02/map/index.html?source=rss&aim=/opinion/keillor>*.

3. Online periodicals with no posting date

ALN, AFN. "Title of Article."
　　<u>Title of Online Publication</u>. n.d.
　　Access Date <url>.

Power, Matthew. "Hiking the Great Wall: Astride the Dragon's Back." <u>National Geographic.com</u>. n.d. 8 Sept. 2007 <*http://www.nationalgeographic.com/adventure/0510/features/hiking_great_wall.html>*.

II. In-Text Citations

As with APA in-text citations, the purpose of MLA in-text citations is for the reader to be able to find the source in the Works Cited list. Therefore, each citation must correspond to an entry in the Works Cited list. The MLA form for in-text citations is the author(s) last name(s) followed by the page number(s). Below is a sample Works Cited list and the corresponding in-text citation for each entry.

Works Cited

Charleston, Rita. "Moscow Offers History, Art—and McDonald's." <u>Philadelphia Tribune</u> 7 Oct. 2007: T26-T29.

De Geus, Piet. "From the Slovenian Alps to Lake Balaton. <u>Off the Beaten Track</u> (n.d.) 9 Sept. 2007 <http://www.off-the-beaten-track.net/>.

"The Heart and Soul of Morocco." <u>The Week</u> 13 July 2007: 34.

Schultz, Patricia. <u>1000 Places to See Before You Die</u>. New York: Workman Publishing Company, Inc., 2003.

In-Text Citations

The basic citation is the author's last name followed by the page number.
(Charleston T27)

Since Web pages typically do not have page numbers, cite the source with the author's last name.
(De Geus)

If there is no author, use an abbreviated title with a comma in quotation marks followed by the year.
("The Heart," 2007)

If you directly quote from a source, you need to indicate the page number.
(Schultz 384)

III. Guidelines for Research Paper Format

1. Use double spacing throughout your paper. Do not add extra spacing between paragraphs.

2. Use a 12-point font. Acceptable fonts are Times New Roman and Courier New.

3. In the heading section of each page, use right justification and put your last name and the page number.

Sanchez 1

4. On the first page of your paper, put your name, your instructor's name, the name of the class and the date in the upper left-hand corner of the page. Skip a line and center the title. Skip another line, and begin writing your introductory paragraph.

Sanchez 1

Leandro Sanchez
Professor Marsh
English 101
29 February 2008

The Dangers of Sleeping Pills

Every day we are flooded with stimuli from electronic

sources: MP3 players, cell phones, and computers. There are

televisions, DVD players, radios, and video games keeping us

occupied at home. At night, it is no wonder that when stimuli

5. If your instructor requires a title page, center your title at about one third of the page down. Skip two lines, and center your name. At the bottom of the page, center the name of the class, the instructor's name, and the date.

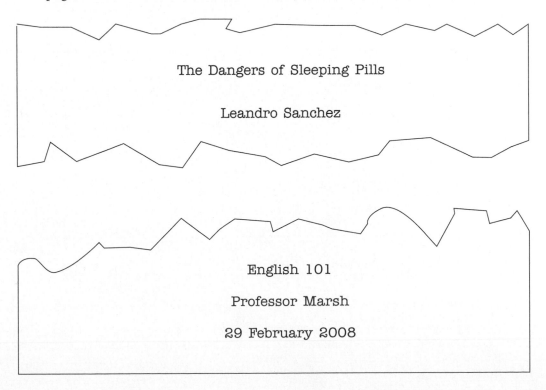

The Dangers of Sleeping Pills

Leandro Sanchez

English 101

Professor Marsh

29 February 2008

6. If your paper has a title page, start the heading on the page after the title page and center the title of your paper, and begin your introductory paragraph on the (double-spaced) line.

Sanchez 1

The Dangers of Sleeping Pills

Every day we are flooded with stimuli from electronic sources: MP3 players, cell phones, and computers. There are televisions, DVD players, radios, and video games keeping us occupied at home. At night, it is no wonder that when stimuli

7. Your Works Cited list should be on a separate page.

INDEX